Barry

PREPARING FOR ADOLESCENCE

- Gives the facts about menstruation, masturbation, venereal disease and other topics teens sometimes are afraid to ask about.

- Takes a close look at the ten most common misconceptions teenagers have about love.

- Offers solid advice on overcoming feelings of inferiority—and helping others over the same bridge.

- Includes a special chapter in which four teenagers talk frankly and openly about their own experience.

DR. JAMES DOBSON is a frequent guest on TV talk shows such as the "Dinah Shore Show," Tom Snyder's "Tomorrow Show" and Barbara Walters's "Not for Women Only." His bestselling books include *Dare to Discipline, The Strong-Willed Child, Hide or Seek,* and *What Wives Wish Their Husbands Knew About Women.*

Associate Clinical Professor of Pediatrics at the University of Southern California School of Medicine, Dr. Dobson also serves at Children's Hospital in Los Angeles.

Bantam Books by Dr. James Dobson

DARE TO DISCIPLINE
PREPARING FOR ADOLESCENCE

Preparing
for
Adolescence

by
Dr. James Dobson

BANTAM BOOKS
TORONTO · NEW YORK · LONDON · SYDNEY

PREPARING FOR ADOLESCENCE

*A Bantam Book / published by arrangement with
Vision House Publishers*

PRINTING HISTORY

Vision House edition published July 1978

Bantam edition / September 1980
2d printing .... December 1980
3rd printing .... July 1981

Bantam Books are published by Bantam Books, Inc. Its trademark, consisting of the words "Bantam Books" and the por-
trayal of a rooster, is Registered in U.S. Patent and Trademark
Office and in other countries. Marca Registrada. Bantam
Books, Inc., 666 Fifth Avenue, New York, New York 10103.

PRINTED IN THE UNITED STATES OF AMERICA

12 11 10 9 8 7 6 5 4

Contents

A Message To Parents

How would you like to be thirteen years old again, by the wave of a magic wand? I can almost hear my adult readers answering that question in one booming voice: "No Thanks!" Everyone in our culture wants to remain young, but not *that* young! And why not? Because we grown-ups remember our adolescent years as the most stressful and threatening time of life.

Most of us recall the scary physical changes that were occurring during those early years. We also remember our sexual anxieties and the guilt that was associated with our strange new desires. We have not forgotten the self-doubt and feelings of inferiority which seemed unbearable at times. And of course, we recall the emotional vulnerability to practically everything throughout adolescense . . . vulnerability to failure, to ridicule, to embarrassment, to parental attitudes, and especially to any form of rejection by members of the opposite sex. There's no doubt about it: adolescence was a turbulent voyage for most of us "old folks" (i.e., those over thirty!).

From this perspective, it does seem strange that we parents are so reluctant to share our youthful experiences with our own children. Preteenagers could

1

profit from what we have learned *because we've been where they're going.* Nevertheless, we typically keep our memories to ourselves and permit our boys and girls to sail into the same troubled waters with no preparation or orientation or warning. The result is often disastrous. As I stated in a previous publication, "The primary reason adolescence is so distressing is because youngsters do not fully understand what is happening to them. Many of their fears and anxieties and discouragements could be obviated by a simple instructional program."*

Where would such an educational effort begin, and what content would it cover? The book which you hold in your hand is addressed to those questions. It was written specifically for boys and girls between ten and fifteen years of age, and is expressed in language that they can understand. This book describes the typical "adolescent experience" and discusses the delicate issues without flinching, including masturbation, menstruation, sexual morality, parent-child conflict, drug abuse, conformity, and, most importantly, the "canyon of inferiority."

The final chapter may be the most beneficial, which was taken from a recorded conversation with four teenagers. These young people participated in an open discussion designed to explain to younger readers what they can expect to feel and experience in the years ahead. That recorded session, which took place in my home, was a meaningful time of sharing feelings and fears and hopes and dreams. I think your child will find the text interesting and helpful.

Not only was the final chapter taken from a tape recording, but this entire book originally appeared in the form of a cassette tape album by the same name. The six tapes in the *Preparing for Adolescence* album represent quiet conversations between my listeners and me, with one cassette being devoted to each of

*Hide or Seek, Fleming H. Revell, 1974, p. 108.

the six chapters in the book. The album is available through bookstores (or can be ordered from the address provided on the final page of this text). Also available is a *Preparing for Adolescence Growth Pak*, which includes the six tapes, this book, a workbook for students, and two instructional tapes addressed to parents.

Let me conclude this statement by citing an analogy. Each September, football coaches across America bring together the boys they hope to mold into a team. They drill the players on fundamentals—on blocking, tackling, throwing, and catching. For two weeks or more, this grueling practice continues day after day. Finally, the night of the game arrives amidst tension and expectation. The stadium is filled with screaming fans and the opponents are waiting on the field. Before leaving the locker room, however, the coach gathers his team for one last reminder and word of encouragement. You see, he knows that there will be little opportunity to teach or guide once the game has begun. His final words are vitally important, and in fact could even change the outcome of the game. After his remarks have been delivered, he sends his team out to do its best.

A parent who is preparing his child for adolescence is functioning much like that football coach. Since childhood he has been systematically teaching the "fundamentals"—getting the youngster ready for the approaching contest. They drilled and practiced throughout the elementary school years, continuing into junior high. They rehearsed the proper spiritual attitudes and moral values and they worked especially hard on building self-confidence. Finally the moment of truth arrives, and a concluding instructional session is held.

"Don't forget what we've been teaching you," Dad says.

"Watch out for the tackler I told you about," warns Mom.

"Do a good job, son. We believe in you!" they both shout.

Junior nods affirmatively and runs onto the field. His parents stand glassy-eyed on the sidelines, knowing that their coaching job is almost over. They have made their contribution, and the outcome now depends on the bony kid in the backfield.

Do you get the message? If you have a youngster in the preadolescent age, you should capitalize on this final "coaching session" prior to the big game. You must take this occasion to refresh his memory, provide last-minute instructions, and offer any necessary words of caution. But beware: if you let this fleeting moment escape unnoticed, you may never get another opportunity.

Preparing for Adolescence was designed to help with that important assignment, and I'm confident that you will handle it properly. Knute Rockne would be proud of you!

James C. Dobson, Ph.D.

1

The Secret of Self-Esteem

You are about to read a very personal book about an important time of life known as adolescence . . . those years between childhood and adulthood. Some of you are nine, ten, or eleven years old now, and you're just beginning to think about growing up. You're not sure what's coming, but you're excited about the experience and want to know more about the details. This book is written for you.

Others of you are already teenagers, and these concepts will be important for you too. Whether you're looking forward to your teen years or are already involved in them, you'll soon understand a little more about the questions and problems that are likely to occur in the years immediately ahead.

But why make such a big deal about adolescence? Why should we go to the effort to learn about this period of life? Well, very honestly, growing up will not be the easiest thing you'll ever do. It was not easy for those who are now adults, and you won't find it simple either. It's always difficult to grow up, because life presents many new demands when you enter a new phase. You don't remember it, I'm sure, but before you were born you were curled up nice and cozy inside your mother's warm body. You could hear her heart beating steady, soft, and secure, and you were safe and warm and comfortable in that world that God had provided. All your needs were met and there wasn't a care in the world. You had nothing to worry about and not a single concern.

But when the proper time came, you were rudely pushed out of that perfect little pocket, whether you liked it or not (nobody asked you!), and you entered this cold world where a doctor picked you up by your heels and whacked your behind. (That was some kind of welcome for a new fellow in the neighborhood!)

As a matter of fact, while you were hanging there, looking at all those upside-down people all around you for the first time, you probably would rather have gone back to that protected little world you just came from. But you simply couldn't stay in your mother's womb if you were going to grow and develop and learn.

The Challenge of Adolescence

In a way, moving into adolescence is like that. You've been in the very warm, secure world of childhood. All your needs have been met by your parents: they were there to put a Band-Aid on your big toe when you stubbed it on a rock, and they kissed away your tears when things didn't go right. You played most of the time, and life was pretty rosy and comfortable. But you can't stay in that childhood world forever, any more than you could remain in your mother's body. There's something better ahead for you—the excitement of growing up, of becoming an adult, of having your own family, of earning your own living, of making your own decisions, of being independent. This is the natural, necessary process of moving from childhood to adulthood.

Unfortunately, however, you can't just *suddenly* mature. First you have to wiggle out of your secure world of childhood, and that is where the difficulty often begins. There will be times when life will whack you on the behind, so to speak, just as it did before. And you may even feel that you're hanging by your heels once in awhile. There will be some new fears and some new problems, and the world won't be quite as safe as it used to be. But it's an exciting world, and it will be even better if you know what to expect.

With that introduction, then, I want to describe some of the new experiences that are about to occur. You'll soon have some of the most thrilling moments of your life (and some of the scariest, too!). We will be talking about the things that teenagers worry about most—the events that are most often upsetting. I want to help you get better acquainted with your mind, with your feelings, with your emotions, with your attitudes, with your body, with your hopes and dreams, with who you are, with where you're going, with how to get there, and with the things you're likely to face in the years ahead. We are going to face these issues head-on; nothing will be considered too sensitive or too delicate to discuss, as long as it's relevant to those of you between twelve and twenty years of age.

As you read this book, I hope it will make you want to discuss these issues further with someone in whom you have confidence. Let this be just a beginning; start to ask your own questions, to express your own concerns, and to make growing up a very personal event in your life.

The Dark Canyon

Let's begin by playing a mental game for a moment. Imagine yourself driving alone down the highway in a small car. You've just come through a little town by the name of Puberty, but now you're back on the main highway, and over on the right you see a sign that says "Adultsville, eight years straight ahead." You're clipping along the highway at about 55 miles an hour, heading for this great new city that you've heard so much about.

But as you round a curve, you suddenly see a man waving a red flag and holding up a warning sign. He motions for you to stop as quickly as possible, so you jam on the brakes and skid to a halt just in front of the flagman. He comes over to the window of your car and says, "Friend, I have some very important information for you. A bridge has collapsed about one mile down the road, leaving a huge drop-off into a dark canyon. If you're not careful, you'll drive your car off the edge of the road and tumble down that canyon, and, of course, if you do that you'll never get to Adultsville."

No Backing Up

So what are you going to do? You can't back up because your car has no reverse gear. *None* of the cars that travel on this highway can go backward. That's like trying to back up on the freeway—it just can't be done. So you ask the flagman, "What am I going to do?" and he says, "Well, I have this suggestion for you. Go ahead and drive down the road, but go slowly and carefully and keep watching for this ruined bridge. When you get to it, turn to the right and go south for about a mile or two. Then you'll find a place where you can get around the canyon and back onto the main highway again. You don't have to fall down that hole—you can drive around it—so good luck and drive carefully."

Now let me explain the meaning of this story. The automobile you're driving represents your own life. It has your name on the door. In fact, it has all of your characteristics, and you're driving this sports car down the highway of life toward adulthood. And you see, I am that flagman standing beside the road. I'm waving the banner back and forth, and holding up a warning sign, and motioning for you to stop. I want to warn you about a problem that lies down the road—a "canyon" that *most* teenagers fall into on the road to adulthood. This is not a problem that affects just a few teenagers; nearly everybody has to deal with it one way or another during the adolescent years.

After I've motioned you to stop, I lean in the window of your car and tell you that many other young people have wrecked their lives by plunging down this dark gorge, but I can show you how to avoid it— how to go around the danger.

The Agony of Inferiority

But what is this problem which so many adolescents face at this time of life? What is it that causes so much hurt and pain to young people between twelve and twenty years of age? It's a feeling of hopelessness that we call "inferiority." It's that awful awareness that nobody likes you, that you're not as good as other people, that you're a failure, a loser, a personal disaster; that you're ugly, or unintelligent, or don't have as much ability as someone else. It's that depressing feeling of worthlessness.

What a shame that *most* teenagers decide they are without much human worth when they're between thirteen and fifteen years of age! It may have happened to some of you even earlier, but in most cases the problem is at its worst during the junior high years. This is the canyon I was talking about—that dark hole in the roadway to adulthood that captures so many young people.

Recently I was interviewed by the editors of *Teen* magazine for an article they were writing on the subject of inferiority. The editors of this magazine knew that most teenagers face this problem. I tried to tell their readers that this is an unnecessary crisis: you can go around the difficulty and avoid it if you know what to expect. But if you simply drive your car down the highway full speed ahead, without thinking about the dangers and without being aware of them, you too can fall victim to this same feeling of worthlessness. It doesn't make sense that we should all have to suffer the agony of defeat. We *all* have human worth, yet so many young people conclude that they're somehow different—that they're truly inferior—that they lack the necessary ingredients for dignity and worth.

Ronny's Problem

Some of you know that I often work with young people who have these kinds of problems (as well as physical problems). I've been on the staff of a children's hospital for ten years. But I previously served on a high school campus, and there I worked with many teenagers who were struggling with some of the feelings that I've been describing to you.

One day I was walking across the grounds of the high school after the bell had rung. Most of the students were already back in class, but I saw a boy coming toward me in the main hall. I knew that his name was Ronny and that he was in his third year of high school. However, I didn't know him very well. Ronny was one of those many students who remain back in the crowd, never calling attention to themselves and never making friends with those around them. It's easy to forget they're alive because they never allow anybody to get acquainted with them.

When Ronny was about fifteen feet away from me, I saw that he was very upset about something. It was obvious that he was distressed, because his face revealed his inner turmoil. As he came a few feet closer, he saw that I was watching him intently. Our eyes locked for a moment, then he looked at the floor as he came closer.

When Ronny and I were parallel, he suddenly

covered his face with both hands and turned toward the wall. His neck and ears turned red, and he began to sob and weep. He was not just crying—he seemed to explode with emotion. I put my arm around him and said, "Can I help you, Ronny? Do you feel like talking to me?" He nodded affirmatively, and I practically had to lead him into my office.

I offered Ronny a chair and closed the door, and I gave him a few minutes to get control of himself before asking him to speak. Then he began to talk to me.

He said, "I've been going to school in this district for eight years, but in all that time I've never managed to make one single friend! Not one. There's not a soul in this high school who cares whether I live or die. I walk to school by myself and I walk home alone. I don't go to football games; I don't go to basketball games or any school activities because I'm embarrassed to sit there all by myself. I stand alone at snack time in the morning, and I eat lunch out in a quiet corner of the campus. Then I go back to class by myself. I don't get along with my dad, and my mother doesn't understand me, and I fight with my sister. And I have nobody! My phone never rings. I have no one to talk to. Nobody knows what I feel and nobody cares. Sometimes I think I just can't stand it anymore!"

Ronny Is Not Alone

I can't tell you how many students have expressed these same feelings to me. One eighth-grade girl named Charlotte felt so badly about herself and about being unpopular that she didn't want to live anymore. She came to school one day and told me she had taken all the pills that were available in the medicine cabinet in an attempt to do away with herself. But she didn't really want to die, or else she wouldn't have told me what she had done. She was actually calling for help. The school nurse and I got her to the hospital just in time to save her life. Both Charlotte and Ronny are among many thousands of students who are overwhelmed by their own worthlessness, and sometimes this even takes away their desire to live.

Some young people feel inferior and foolish only occasionally, such as when they fail at something very important. But others feel worthless *all* the time. Maybe you're one of those individuals who hurts every day. Have you ever had that big lump in your throat that comes when you feel that nobody cares— that nobody likes you—that maybe they even hate you? Have you ever wished that you could crawl out of your skin and get into another person's body? Do you ever feel like a complete dummy when you're in a group? Would you ever like to descend into a hole and disappear? If you've ever had those kinds of feelings, I hope you'll finish reading this book, because it's for *you*! I wish Ronny and Charlotte could have read what I'm writing when they expressed such feelings. I wish they could have recognized their true worth as human beings. They had, you see, driven into the canyon of inferiority and were groping in the darkness below.

Why?

Now let's ask a very important question. Why do so many teenagers feel inferior? Why can't American young people grow up liking themselves? Why is it common for people to examine themselves and be bitterly disappointed with the person God has made them? Why is it necessary for everyone to bump his head on the same old rock? These are very good questions, and I believe there are good answers to them.

Mother Nature's Damage

As young people grow up in our American society today, there are three things that teenagers feel they *must* have in order to feel good about themselves. The first of these, and by far the most important, is physical attractiveness. Did you know that about 80 percent of the teenagers in our society don't like the way they look? *Eighty percent!*

If you asked ten teenagers what they are most unhappy about, eight of them would be dissatisfied with some feature of their bodies. They feel ugly and unattractive, and they think about that problem most of the time. They also believe that the opposite sex doesn't like them. The girls feel too tall and the boys feel too short, or they feel too fat or too thin or they're worried about the pimples on their faces or about the freckles on their noses or the color of their hair, or they think their feet are too big or they don't like their fingernails.

No matter how minor the problem is, it can create great anxieties and depression. Most teenagers examine themselves carefully in the mirror to see how much damage has been done by Mother Nature, and they don't like what they see. Since none of us is perfect, they usually find something about themselves that they don't like. Then they worry and fret about it, wishing they didn't have that flaw. Can you imagine being depressed and miserable over something as silly as having a nose that is a fraction of an inch longer than you think it should be?

What Kind of "Friends"?

One reason teenagers become so sensitive about their tiny flaws is because their "friends" have teased and embarrassed them during their early years. Unfortunately, boys and girls are often brutal to one another, hurling insults back and forth like poison darts. I knew a third-grade girl, for example, who received a note at school from another girl who apparently hated her. She had done nothing unkind to the writer of the note, but this is what it said:

> Awful Janet
>
> Your the stinkest girl in this world. I hope you die but of course I suppose that's impossible. I've some ideals.
>
> 1. Play in the road
> 2. Cut your throad
> 3. Drink poison
> 4. Get drunk
> 5. Knife yourself
>
> Please do some of this you big fat Girl. we all hate you. I'm praying Oh please lord let Janet die. Were in need of fresh air. Did you hear me lord cause if you didn' will all die with her here. See Janet we're not all bad.
>
> from Wanda Jackson*

Have you ever received a note like that? More important, have you ever *written* that kind of note? Young people are easily hurt, and the pain from this kind of message goes very deep and lasts a long time. It may even be remembered after Janet is grown.

"Pee Wee" and "Gorilla"

One of the most damaging games played by teenagers is to create unkind nicknames that draw attention to anything different or unusual about a person. In this way they put a spotlight on the feature that the victim most wants to hide. You may have been given a

*Quoted from *Hide or Seek*, Revell Publishers, 1974. Used by permission.

nickname or teased about your body at some time or another. If you're a small boy you may have been called "Runt" or "Pee Wee." If you're a big girl you may have been called "Moose" or "Gorilla." If you have large ears they may have called you "Dumbo." You see, *no one* has a perfect body and *everyone* has something that can be made fun of. Even Farrah Fawcett–Majors, the Hollywood beauty, said recently that she thought her mouth was too large. (I never really noticed.) At least Farrah was able to talk about her imperfections. Most people try to conceal theirs in shame.

To illustrate further, let's suppose that Charlie is a healthy boy, ten years of age. He has a strong body, a sharp mind, and a loving home. He has been blessed by many good things in life, and he experiences very few problems. Then one day a group of students on the playground begins teasing him about his big feet. They call him "Snowshoes" and "Duckfeet." It's all done in fun, I guess, but Charlie takes it very seriously. He becomes extremely sensitive about the size of his feet, and thinks everyone is laughing behind his back. He tries to hide his feet under his desk at school, and insists that his mother buy him shoes that are three sizes too small. Eventually, Charlie may become depressed and disinterested in living instead of being a happy fellow who enjoys the advantages God has given him. This illustration may sound unreal to you, but please believe me, I know many "Charlies" who have been made to dislike themselves over very minor flaws.

If you're not yet a teenager you should know that you're likely to be dissatisfied with your body in the future. If your concern is great, it may cause you to be shy or very easily embarrassed. Or it may lead you to be the opposite—loud and angry—because you feel foolish and you think nobody likes you anyway. There's just no way to estimate the amount of pain and worry that teenagers feel over the way they look.

At Seventeen

This concern was expressed in the words of a popular song written by Janis Ian. She actually won a Grammy Award in 1976 for this song entitled "At Seventeen."* The words are reproduced below so that you can see how feelings of inferiority are reflected throughout this song.

> I learned the truth at seventeen
> That love was meant for beauty queens
> And high school girls with clear-skinned smiles
> Who married young and then retired.
>
> The valentines I never knew,
> The Friday-night charades of youth,
> Were spent on one more beautiful;
> At seventeen I learned the truth.
>
> And those of us with ravaged faces
> Lacking in the social graces
> Desperately remained at home,
> Inventing lovers on the phone
> Who called to say, "Come dance with me,"
> And murmured vague obscenities.
> It isn't all it seems at seventeen.
>
> To those of us who knew the pain
> Of valentines that never came
> And those whose names were never called
> When choosing sides for basketball.
>
> It was long ago and far away;
> The world was younger than today
> And dreams were all they gave for free
> To ugly-duckling girls like me.

I am not personally acquainted with Janis Ian, but I'm sure of one very important fact about her: she too has been down in the canyon of inferiority. It would have been impossible for her to write the words of this song without having felt inadequate when she was younger. She speaks for millions when she describes "those of us with ravaged faces" (those with pimples and blackheads) and "those whose names were never called when choosing sides for basketball." I hope *you* will never be included in this vast group of discouraged people who learn so many painful lessons "at seventeen."

Who's Dumb?

The second characteristic that young people don't like about themselves is that they feel unintelligent (or dumb). This feeling often begins during the very early school years, when they have trouble learning in school. Either they have a hard time learning to read, and they start worrying about this problem, or else they blurt out answers that cause everyone to laugh. They gradually start to believe that everybody in the classroom (including the teacher) thinks they're stupid, and this brings the same old feelings of inferiority.

The more often a student fails in school, the more discouraged he is likely to become. He will probably be called unkind names by his classmates, such as "Stupid" or "Dummy" or "Lamebrain." If these insults are too painful, he may lose all interest in school and even quit trying. This causes a vicious cycle to develop: his refusal to work results in more failure, which brings more ridicule in the classroom, which produces less motivation to try, which results in further failure . . . and round and round it goes. Finally this individual reaches the awful conclusion that he has a defective brain and is certain to fail throughout life. It is a terrible experience to believe that you have no human worth.

Parents, too, can accidentally make their children feel they aren't very smart. Adults are human beings too, and they get impatient and tired, just like you do. This may cause them to become upset and call their children insulting names, which are remembered for a lifetime.

So children often grow up thinking they're stupid and dumb, and this is the second reason why inferiority is so common among junior high and high school students.

The Measure of Money

The third value that young people use to measure their worth is money. You see, they think the wealthy family is more important than the poor one, and to be accepted and popular they have to dress a certain way, or their family has to have a particular kind of car, or they have to live in a big house in the right part of town, or their father has to have a certain kind of job. The young person who can't afford these things sometimes feels inferior and inadequate. Everybody else has sweaters to wear, but he has to wear shirts that are worn around the edges. This financial problem is not as common now as it used to be, simply because today more people have the necessities of life. However, some families still live in poverty, and those children who can't afford to be like their friends sometimes feel inferior because they are poor.

Beauty, intelligence, and money are the three attributes valued most highly in our society. And when junior high students first discover that they are lacking in one (or all three) of these characteristics, they begin sliding downward in despair. For them, the "bridge" has collapsed and a dark canyon looms below.

Now if you're one of those young people who *al-*

ready feels bad about life—if you feel miserable about yourself and would like to escape somehow, to just run away from it all, or if you've been hurt when someone said unkind words, let me give you several suggestions that may help you.

1. Recognize that you are not alone.

First, begin observing the people around you and see if you detect hidden feelings of inferiority. When you go to school tomorrow, quietly watch the students who are coming and going. Some will be smiling and laughing and talking and carrying their books and playing baseball. Unless you take a second look, you'd never know they had a care in the world. But I assure you, many of them have the same concerns that trouble you. They reveal these doubts by being very shy and quiet, or by being extremely angry and mean, or by being silly, or by being afraid to participate in a game or contest, or by blushing frequently, or by acting proud and "stuck-up." You'll soon learn to recognize the signs of inferiority, and then you'll know that it is a *very* common disorder! Once you fully comprehend that others feel as you do, then you *should never again* feel alone. It will give you more confidence to know that everyone is afraid of embarrassment and ridicule—that we're all sitting in the same leaky boat, trying to plug the watery holes. And would you believe, *I* nearly drowned in that same leaky boat when I was fourteen years old?

2. Face your problem.

The second suggestion that I hope will be helpful for you is to face the issue of what's bugging you. Look squarely at the thought that keeps gnawing at you from the back of your mind or from deep within your heart, causing a black cloud to hang over your head day and night. It would be a good idea to get alone, where there is no one to interfere with your thoughts. Then *list* all the things which you most dislike about yourself. Nobody is going to see this paper except the people to whom you choose to show it, so you can be completely honest. Write down everything that has been bothering you. Even admit the characteristics that you dislike, including the tendency to get mad and blow up (if that applies to you).

Identify your most serious problems as best as possible. Do you get frustrated and angry at people and then feel bad later? Or is it your shyness that makes you afraid when you're with other people? Or is it your inability to express your ideas—to put your thoughts into words? Is it your laziness or your unkindness to other people, or the way you look? Whatever concerns you, write it down as best you can. (You're probably going to need a big stack of paper, because most people can find too many things they don't like about themselves.) Withhold nothing from this writing assignment. Then when you're finished, go back through the list and put a checkmark by those items that worry you the most—the problems that you spend the most time thinking and fretting about.

Find a True Friend

Now you're ready to take some action to improve your circumstances. It would be a good idea to select someone you trust, a person in whom you have confidence. This should be an adult who understands the problems of young people. Perhaps it will be your parent—or your teacher or counselor or pastor. You will know the right person. Take your list to that trusted leader and go over it with him or her, discussing each one of your problems. Talk openly about your feelings, asking your friend to make suggestions about changing the things that concern you.

It is very likely that many of the problems you face have been conquered by other people, and you may be able to profit from their experience also. In other words, there could be an easy solution available. Maybe you don't have to go through life struggling with the same concerns that have troubled other people. Your first step, then, is to map a strategy, a plan of action, a way of solving your problems. You'll feel much better for having discussed your worries openly, and you just might discover some successful solution.

The Fire of Commitment

But how will you handle the remaining items on your list that can't be changed? What can you do with the more difficult problems that defy solution? *It would be wise to remember that the best way to have a healthy mind is to learn to accept those things which you cannot change.* There will always be circumstances which we wish we could rearrange or remove. However, the happiest people in the world are not those who have no problems, but the people who have learned to live with those things that are less than perfect.

Let me suggest, then, that you take your remaining list of "unsolvable problems" to a private place where a small fire will not be dangerous. Perhaps you would like to have your counselor-friend present for this ceremony. Then burn that paper as a symbol to God that the problems are now His. Your prayers should contain this message to Him (stated in your own words):

Dear Jesus, I am bringing all my problems and worries to you tonight, because you are my best friend. You already know about my strengths and weaknesses, because You made me. That's why I'm burning this paper now. It's my way of saying that I'm giving my life to you . . . with my good qualities along with my shortcomings and failures. I'm asking you to use me in whatever way You wish. Make me the kind of person You want me to be. And from this moment forward, I'm not going to worry about my imperfections.

God Knows and Cares

I'm sure that you will find great warmth, love, and acceptance from God when you pray that prayer. By doing so, you are saying, "I want Your will for my life, not because I'm a superstar or superman or superwoman, but because You promised to help those who admit their weaknesses. I'm depending on *Your* power and *Your* strength to make something beautiful out of my life." The Bible teaches us to reveal this humble dependence on the Lord, and He will honor it!

Did you know that God sees you when you hurt? He knows those deep fears and frustrations that you thought no one understood. He knows the longings of your heart, and He's always there during those moments when a little tear pushes out of your eye and down your cheek . . . those times when you feel totally alone. In fact, God loves you and me so much that He actually sent His only Son to die for us. Now that's real love at its greatest! I'm convinced that Jesus would have died for me (or you) even if I had been the only individual in the whole world. That's how much He cares for us.

If God can love us that much, just the way we are, why can't we accept ourselves? That's probably the best question of the year.

Something Beautiful, Something Good

Bill Gaither has written a song with the words, "Something beautiful, something good; all my confusion He understood. All I had to offer Him was brokenness and strife, but He made something beautiful of my life." God can do that with *your* life. If you read the Bible—and I hope you do—you'll learn that God does not choose the superstars and the miracle men to do His work. All through the ages He has selected ordinary people with human flaws, people who were less than perfect, to do His jobs. When Jesus was choosing His disciples He didn't select the most powerful and popular men in the country at that time. He chose ordinary fishermen, and even a tax collector who was hated in his community.

Send Somebody Else

You may also remember the story of Moses and his experience with the burning bush as told in the book of Exodus. God was speaking to Moses through the bush and said something like this: "Moses, I have a very important job for you to do. I want you to tell Pharaoh that I have commanded him to let my people go."

Well, Moses felt inferior and inadequate, just as so many people do today. He gave this kind of answer to the Lord: "God, couldn't You send somebody else? When I get to Pharaoh's palace I know they're going to laugh at me. They could even throw me into prison. I think, Lord, that perhaps you ought to send somebody else." And then Moses told God what was *actually* bothering him—he admitted the reason he felt inferior: "And besides, Lord, I didn't want to bring this up, but you know that I stutter. I'm not eloquent of speech . . . my words don't come out right. When I try to talk at an important moment, the words get all tangled up. Lord, I'm not the man for the job. I'd rather stay home, if you don't mind."

In the fourteenth verse of the fourth chapter of Exodus, the Bible says, "The anger of the Lord was kindled against Moses." The Lord was displeased at Moses for using inferiority as an excuse. You see, God intended to go with Moses and help him. That's why He didn't want Moses to hide behind an excuse of inferiority. The Lord doesn't want *you* to use this excuse of inferiority either, because He will help you to accomplish what He tells you to do. When you return to school tomorrow and find yourself afraid of other students—afraid they're going to laugh at you or leave you out—just remember that you're not by yourself. You have with you the power of the God who created the entire universe. He can make something beautiful of your life, if you'll allow Him to take charge.

3. Compensate for your weaknesses.

Are you ready for the third suggestion? There's a very important word that you ought to understand, and it's called *compensation.* Compensation may be a ten-dollar word, but it has a very simple meaning. It means *to make up for your weaknesses by concentrating on your strengths*—in other words, to *compensate* for your weaknesses. Returning to the unsolvable problems on your list which bother you the most, you can *balance* those weak areas by excelling in some other abilities.

Not everybody can be the best-looking person in school. If this is your situation, say "All right, so what? There are a lot of other people in the same boat, and it doesn't really matter. My worth doesn't depend on the arrangement of my body. I'll put my effort into something that will help me feel good about myself. I'll be the best trumpet player in the band, or I'll succeed in my part-time job, or I'll raise rabbits for fun and profit, or I'll make good grades in school, or I'll see how many friends I can make, or I'll learn how to play basketball as well as possible, or I'll become a good pianist or drummer, or I'll just see how pleasant a personality I can develop (that's one that nearly everybody can work on), or I'll learn to play tennis, or I'll become a seamstress, or I'll draw or paint and express myself through art, or I'll write poetry or short stories, or I'll become a good cook." Or maybe you could become highly skilled at entertaining small children and become well-trained as a child-care worker.

You see, there's success waiting for *you* if you'll just look for it. You can learn to make the most out of what you have, and that's the first step toward developing self-confidence and acceptance. It doesn't hurt nearly as much to be rejected by other people when you know that you're successful at doing something. So develop a skill that will make you proud of yourself, and gradually you will start to have a better self-concept. You will begin to like yourself a bit more, and when you like yourself better, so will other people.

4. Have genuine friends.

This brings us to the fourth suggestion: *nothing helps your self-confidence more than genuine friends.* When you know that other people like you, it's much easier to accept yourself. You don't have to be beautiful or highly intelligent or wealthy in order to be liked by other people. "The best way to *have* a friend is to *be* a good friend to others." That's a very old proverb, but it's still very true.

How can you make new friends quickly and easily? You must remember that the people you deal with every day have exactly the same problems I've been discussing with you. Understanding that fact will help you know how to get along with them and earn their respect. Never make fun of other people or ridicule them. Let them know that you respect and accept them, and that they are important to you. Make a conscious effort to show this kind of affection for people.

But you can't be a phony about showing respect to others; it has to be real. People will see right through you if you're phony. Learn to protect the reputation of other people, and they will do the same for you. Be sensitive to their feelings; they have the same needs that you do. Be kind to them; don't ever be sarcastic or catty. You may think you're getting away with insulting other people or laughing at their mis-

takes. But you'll get it back; they won't forget your
insults. They may not hit you in the nose (or maybe
they will!), and they may not cry or run away, and
they may not even say anything when you treat them
unkindly. But they'll probably try to hurt you in return the next time they have a chance. They'll gossip
about you or try to get other people not to like you.

Friendship Pays

Fortunately, the opposite is also true. When
you've befriended someone, they will remember your
generosity and look for ways to return your kindness.
You'll be surprised at how many friends you can make
by being understanding, by "covering" for other people when they make a mistake, by standing up for
them when others are trying to make them feel foolish. You'll find that this sensitivity leads to friendship,
which leads to greater self-confidence.

One of the most important responsibilities in the
Christian life is to care about other people—to smile at
them and to be a friend of the friendless. You see,
God wants to use you to help His other children who
feel inferior. He said, "Inasmuch as you do it to the
least of these my brethren, you are doing it unto me!"
If you'll start living this kind of Christian life as rec-
ommended in the Bible, I know you'll find that your
own self-confidence will grow, and that God will
bless you for it. The Lord honors those who obey
Him.

God's Values

Let me stress again that the attributes which our
society values most highly—beauty, intelligence, and
money—must be seen from the Christian point of
view. These are *man's* values, but not *God's* values.
The Lord doesn't measure your worth the way people

do. He emphasizes in His Word that each of us is worth more than the possessions of the *entire* world. This is true just because we are human beings—not because of the way we look, or to whom we are married, or what our parents do, or how much money we have, or how much we have accomplished in life. Those earthly factors don't make the difference at all.

Did you know that the Bible tells us that God actually hates the three things which our world values most highly? Luke 16:15 states, "For that which is highly esteemed among men is abomination in the sight of God." He despises those things which we treasure, because they get in the way of our self-confidence, and they interfere with the work we ought to be doing for Him. Those phony values could keep you from being a good parent or employee or business person. More importantly, these false values can interfere with your Christian life, making you feel that even God doesn't accept you as a person. The temporary values of beauty, intelligence, and money represent a method of estimating human worth, and that's why God hates them. His method gives eternal worth to every one of us, and that includes *you* and *me*!

In summary, I must speak to those of you who have not yet suffered from feelings of inferiority. I hope you will remember my illustration of driving a car down the road. You don't have to fall into that black hole; you don't have to tumble into the canyon with all the other wrecked cars at the bottom. You can drive around this dangerous drop-off. Don't let it happen to you. Don't listen to the little voice inside you which says, "You're not really worthy; you're a failure; there's something wrong with you; you're ugly; there's something wrong with your mind; you're different; everyone is laughing at you; they think you're a fool; you're going to be a failure in life; everything will go wrong."

Don't believe it! Steer your car around the canyon of inferiority. God will help you do it!

2

Everybody's Doing It

What does the word "conformity" mean to you? Is it just a mysterious word in the dictionary, or does it relate directly to your daily living? Though you may never have used this word before, you'll need to become very familiar with its meaning. It will play an important role during the adolescent period of your life.

The word "conformity" refers to the desire to be just like everyone else—to do what they do and say what they say, to think what they think and wear what they wear. A conformist is someone who is afraid to be different from the majority; he feels a great need to be like everyone else. To conform means to accept the ideas, the fashion, the way of walking, and the way of talking that is popular at the time. In our society, there is *tremendous* pressure on all of us to conform to the standards of the group.

The Orientation Blues

Conformity is not only a problem among adolescents. Let me give you an excellent example of conformity which took place in a group of adults. When I first joined the staff at Childrens Hospital in Los Angeles, I had to go through an "orientation session." An orientation session is a meeting that employees are required to attend when they begin a new job. It's a training period prepared by the employer to acquaint each person with the organization that has hired them. But unfortunately, these meetings are usually boring—it almost seems that they're planned to be dull! The speakers talk endlessly about Blue Cross Insurance and retirement programs and the proper use of the telephone and similar topics that are terribly monotonous. Knowing this, I dreaded going through the orientation session at the hospital.

Nevertheless, I arrived as expected at nine in the morning. There were twelve new employees in the room that day, and it just happened that I was the only man there. The eleven women appeared to be young, and I guessed that most of them were secretaries or clerks, probably starting their first jobs. The atmosphere between the people that morning was "icy." In other words, the women were strangers to each other and they seemed frightened and tense. They came in quietly and sat around a large, horseshoe-shaped table, but no one talked unless spoken to. If one of the young ladies had anything to say, she leaned over and covered her mouth so others would not hear.

The Coffee Hope

I could see that there was one possibility of keeping us all awake for the next two hours, and that was for the director to offer us plenty of coffee—it was our only hope! And sure enough, a large coffeepot was percolating on a table in a corner. However, nothing was said about coffee. I can only guess that the pot had not been plugged in until a few minutes earlier, and it was not ready. However, it was obvious that all eleven women were thinking about that coffeepot, because every time it chugged, they would turn and look at it. What's more, there were colorful donuts arranged on the table, and the aroma filled the room. But the goodies were never mentioned.

The orientation lady stepped to the front of the room and began her long-winded speech. She spoke in a dry, monotonous voice, and attacked the first subject on a 42-item list. She talked for over an hour, but still nothing was said about coffee. The women yawned sleepily, leaned on one elbow, and glanced periodically in the direction of the coffeepot.

Finally, after an endless presentation, the leader said, "Okay, we're going to take a break and get some coffee now." However, she wasn't about to send all eleven ladies to the coffee table at the same time. Instead, she thought she had a better idea. She turned to a lady at one end of the table and said, "How would you like to slip back and get a cup of coffee?"

Well, this young lady was very shy, and she wasn't sure she wanted to be the first to go. She obviously knew that there are many ways a person can get "hurt" doing anything in front of eleven other people. She could trip on her way to the coffee table, or the spigot could stick on the coffeepot, or she could burn herself coming back. I watched her as she looked around the room and considered the risks of accepting the coffee. In a moment, she dropped her eyes and said, "No, thank you, I don't believe I'll have any."

I *knew* she wanted a cup of coffee. What she planned to do, it was clear, was to wait until everybody else had gone to the refreshment table, and then she could quietly get a cup of coffee with no risk!

That way her ego wouldn't be in any danger. I found her amusing, but just watched her quietly from the opposite side of the table where I sat.

The Coffee Terror

The orientation lady then turned to the next girl and said, "Well, okay, how about you? Would you like to have a cup of coffee?"

But you see, the second girl faced all the same risks that scared the first young lady, plus a new one. The group had now "spoken" through that first individual and said, "We're not drinking coffee today." Only one "vote" had been cast, but it was unanimous. This pressure on the second girl was also too great, so she said, "No, thank you." That made the vote two to nothing!

The coffee invitation was then extended to the third girl. "Will you have a cup of coffee?" said the leader.

"No, thank you," said the employee.

The pressure then became enormous. It was clear that no one was expected to drink coffee or eat donuts. To my amazement, all the other women refused the offer of refreshments one at a time. Each said, "No, thanks" when their turn came to reply. But when the invitation was made to me, I said, "I believe I'll have a cup."

Would you believe that when I got up to get my cup of coffee, *eleven women followed me to the table!* I looked over my shoulder and here they came. As a gentleman, I felt I should step back and let the ladies go first, and it took me fifteen minutes to reach the goodies table!

Isn't it amazing how terrified we are of each other? We won't even get a cup of coffee if it's not socially acceptable at a given moment! We're terrified that somebody will laugh at us or ridicule us, or that we might make a mistake in front of others. Even such a completely insignificant thing as getting a cup of coffee can be frightening if we think the rest of the group doesn't want us to do it. This causes us to limit our behavior to those acts which are completely safe and totally beyond ridicule. We do that to eliminate the chance of anyone laughing at us.

The Fear of Flared Pants

This pressure to conform is so strong in some people that they feel uncomfortable if they are different in *any* way at all. If flared pants are "in" for boys, woe to the fellow who doesn't get the message, and wears tapered pants! If a girl walks funny or talks with a lisp, she may be laughed at every day. If Fords and Chevrolets are popular at high school, a person had better not buy a Plymouth. That would be an insult to the entire student body! You see, any little deviation, any change at all in what the group declares "this is what we do," becomes a breach of etiquette. They point at the offender and talk disrespectfully about him, making him feel very uncomfortable.

I want you to understand that this pressure to conform is at its worst during adolescence. That's why teenagers often move in "herds," like a flock of sheep, as we will see.

The Card Game

A team of doctors decided to conduct an experiment to study the ways in which group pressure influences young people. To accomplish this, they invited ten teenagers into a room and told them they were going to evaluate their "perception," in order to learn how well each student could "see" the front of the room from where he sat.

Actually, all the teenagers were very close to the front of the room and everybody could see quite easily. What the doctors were *actually* studying was not the students' eyesight, but the effects of group pressure.

The doctors said, "We're going to hold up some cards at the front of the room. On each card are three lines—Line A, Line B, and Line C—each of a different length. In some cases Line A will be the longest; in other cases Line B will be the longest, and in still other cases Line C will be the longest. Several dozen cards will be shown with the lines in a different order. We'll hold them up and point to Line A, Line B, and Line C on each card. *When we point to the longest line, please raise your hand to show that you know it is longer than the others.*" They repeated the directions to be sure everybody understood, and then raised the first card and pointed to the top line.

The Object of the Game

What one student didn't know was that the other nine had been secretly informed earlier to vote for the *second* longest line. In other words, they were told to vote wrongly.

The doctors held up the first card and pointed to Line A, which was clearly shorter than Line B. At this point, all nine students cooperated in the scheme and raised their hands. The fellow being studied looked around in disbelief. It was obvious that Line B was the longest line, but everybody seemed to think Line A was longer. He later admitted that he thought, "I must not have been listening during the directions. Somehow I missed the point, and I'd better do what everybody else is doing or they'll laugh at me." So he carefully raised his hand with the rest of the group.

Then the researchers explained the directions again: "Vote for the *longest* line; raise your hand when we point to the *longest* line."

It couldn't have been more simple! Then they held up the second card, and again, nine people voted for the wrong line! The confused fellow became more tense over his predicament, but eventually he raised his hand with the group once again. Over and over he voted with the group, even though he knew they were wrong.

This one young man was not unusual. In fact, *more than 75 percent of young people tested behaved that same way. They sat there time after time, saying a short line was longer than a long line!* They simply didn't have the courage to say, "The group is wrong. I can't explain why, but you guys are all confused." A small percentage—only 25 out of 100—had the courage to take their stand against the group, even when the majority was obviously wrong. This is what group pressure does to an insecure person!

The Power of a Friend

Another very interesting characteristic was revealed by this study. *If just one other student* recognized (voted for) the right line, then the chances were greatly improved that the fellow who was being studied would also do what he thought was right. This means that if you have *even one friend* who still stand with you against the group, you probably will have more courage too. But when you're all by yourself, it's pretty difficult to take your stand alone.

Now this raises an interesting question. Why is social pressure so great during adolescence? Why are we so afraid of being rejected by the group? Why must we do what we're told by those of our same age? Why can't we be independent? Well, the answer to these questions goes back to the subject of inferiority.

You see, when you feel worthless and foolish—when you don't like yourself—then you are more frightened by the threat of ridicule or rejection by your friends. You become more sensitive about being laughed at. You lack the confidence to be different. Your problems seem bad enough without making them worse by defying the wishes of the majority. So you dress the way they tell you to dress, and you talk the way they tell you to talk, and all your ideas are the group's ideas. You become afraid to get a cup of coffee, or to raise your hand for what you know is right, or to express any of your own views. Your great desire is to behave in the "safest" way possible. These behaviors all have one thing in common: they result from feelings of inferiority.

Dean Martin once said, "Show me a man who doesn't know the meaning of the word 'fear' and I'll show you a dummy who gets beat up a lot!" In this case, however, it's not really a fear of getting "beat up" but a fear that the group is going to reject you— the fear of not being invited to a party . . . the fear of being disliked . . . the fear of failure.

The Teenage Choirs

If you want to confirm the existence of this conformity, look around you. The next time you hear a teen choir singing in your church or school, look closely at the young people involved. You'll notice that all the girls have exactly the same hair-style! If it's fashionable to have long natural hair, then every girl will comb her hair straight down to her shoulders. There will be *very* few exceptions. Perhaps none of the girls will have the courage to curl her hair. On the other hand, if the popular style is curly, or ratted, or back-combed, all the girls will look exactly the same. It is obvious that they have worked hard to try to look just like their friends.

About a year ago a teen choir was singing "The Battle Hymn of the Republic" in a Miami concert. That is a very emotional song, and a person can get carried away while singing, "Glory, glory, hallelujah! His truth is marching on!" There were about sixty teens in this choir, and as they were singing, one girl in the front row became so emotional that she fainted.

The director saw her fall, but he didn't want to wreck the performance, so he continued to lead his choir. Several adults gathered around the unconscious girl and helped her regain her senses. However, when that one young lady passed out, the possibility of fainting was planted in fifty-nine other impressionable heads. .. About six seconds later another young fellow turned white, then buckled and disappeared from the back row. At that point, the "suggestion" of fainting became even stronger. Each singer was thinking, "Is it going to happen to me? I do feel rather dizzy!"

Sure enough, a third young man sailed off the end of the risers and hit the floor with a thud. Then it began to spread like wildfire . . . numbers four, five, and six! By the time the choir reached the final phrase ("His truth is marching on"), *twenty* kids lay flat on their backs! That is conformity at its peak!

The Pressure of Conformity

This group pressure can be even more ridiculous at times. We adults have been told by television advertisers that we must look exactly alike. We're warned, for example, that "the wethead is dead." That means that nobody uses hair oil anymore, and if you use it as you did during the fifties and sixties, there must be something wrong with you.

Old people are made to feel uncomfortable because they are aging. Isn't that foolish? There are more than four billion people on this earth, and every single one of us is growing older. There isn't a single person on earth who isn't aging! (The moment you stop aging you are in deep trouble!)

Nevertheless, adults are made to feel inferior over the normal signs of aging. This great pressure acts to force us all into identical blocks, making us robots instead of human beings.

Think About the Problem

Now let's think about some important questions. Why will this subject of conformity be important to you as you go into the adolescent years? Can you see any reason why peer pressure could be dangerous to you? Do you see any ways it could get you into trouble a little later? How does conformity hurt you right now? How does it keep you from doing what is right? How could it interfere with your life?

The reason conformity is so dangerous is that it can cause you to do things that you know are wrong. This is what happens when you don't have the courage to be different from your friends.

Can You Say No?

Suppose you're in a car with four other young people, each about fifteen years old. You're driving around at night, looking for fun, when the driver reaches into his pocket and retrieves a bottle with some little red pills in it. He takes one pill and pops it in his mouth, and then hands the bottle to the guy sitting by the door. He laughs and takes a pill before handing the bottle to the three of you in the back seat. You are the last one to be handed the bottle, and all four of your friends have taken the pills.

As it is handed to you, what are you going to say? You know that those capsules are called "reds," and that they are very harmful to the body. You don't want to take them, but you don't want to be laughed at either. You hesitate a moment, which causes the fellow beside you to say, "Come on, sissy. Whatsa matter? You scared? Hey, guys, we've got a mama's boy back here! He's afraid daddy will find out. Who would have thought that Jackie-Boy was a big chicken! Come on, Baby Face. Try it, you'll like it!"

Your hands tremble a bit, and you notice that your palms are moist. Then the other boys begin to tease you too, because they want you to do what they are doing. The pressure is enormous. Your heart is pounding. You don't know what to say. You just feel foolish. Maybe you should just try it once to see what it's like. That probably won't hurt much. So you give in. You pop the pill. What a relief to be one of the boys again!

You'll find that the next time drugs are offered, it'll be a little easier to take them because you've done it before. Then you start getting the habit, and soon you'll be seriously hooked on narcotics, all because of the pressure of conformity. This explains the most important reason why drugs are being used by teenagers every day throughout this country. Thousands of young people are permanently damaging their bodies and their lives this way. The human body is very delicate. It can be easily hurt so that the rest of a person's life is spent in pain. Or if the individual "overdoses" on drugs, he can actually kill himself while trying to have a little fun.

I talked to a thirteen-year-old girl the other day who takes ten to twenty reds every day of her life. Her body is so wracked and ruined from these narcotics that she will never be healthy again. What a *shame* to destroy a youthful body in this way! How unfortunate that she didn't have the courage to reply to the person who first offered her drugs, "Why should I wreck my body? It's the only one I have!"

Other harmful behaviors can also be traced to the pressure of conformity. Why do you suppose teenage alcoholism is such a serious problem in this country? Why else would cigarettes continue to be smoked by young people, even though they know that the habit has been proven to shorten life, contaminate the lungs, increase the risk of cancer, and damage the blood vessels? Why do teenagers pick up that first cigarette and inhale the filthy smoke into their pink lungs? It usually begins by a "friend" offering a weed to someone who has never smoked. He says, "Would you like a puff?" And unfortunately, the nonsmoker lacks the guts to say, "No way!"

The Courage to Lead

It will be helpful for you to think about these issues *before* you face a crisis with your friends. Recognize the fact that they are under the same pressure that you feel. They're tempted to take drugs or smoke or drink for the same reason you are—simply because they're afraid to be different. They're afraid that the next time their admired friend (the one who owns the car) decides to pick up some guys for a joyride, he won't include them because they're not much fun to be with. So he acts like a jellyfish and does something that makes no sense whatever.

How much better it is to show that you have confidence in yourself when the pressure is greatest. You can say, "If you guys want to do something crazy, go ahead. But I think it's stupid!" That's not being childish. That's a way of showing that you have the courage to oppose the group when they're wrong.

I'll tell you something else: most teenagers respect a guy or girl who has the courage to be his own person, even when being mocked and teased. An individual with this kind of confidence often becomes a leader. He has shown that he doesn't feel as inferior as the other followers. He's not made of putty inside. Instead, he has the guts to stand up for what he knows is right.

And one other thing: he is likely to influence others who are looking for that one friend who will increase their confidence. (Remember the experiment with the cards?) He might make it possible for someone else to oppose peer pressure too.

The Pain of a Handicap

The pressure of conformity is not only harmful to young people who take drugs or smoke cigarettes or drink alcohol. It is especially damaging to those teenagers who *can't* be like their friends. In the high school where I served as a counselor, for example, there was a blind student who could not accept the fact that she was different from the other students. Her way of dealing with her blindness was to deny that it existed. She refused the help of a special teacher who was hired to work with her. She wouldn't do the work the teacher gave her to do, nor would she talk to this specialist. She even tried to walk without the use of her white cane or a seeing-eye dog. She put her shoulders back and walked down the sidewalk of the school as though she knew where she was going. One day I saw her heading in the wrong direction, but before I could stop her, she walked right into a post. Nevertheless, she simply refused to feel her way around. You see, this unfortunate young lady just could not accept the fact that she was different from "normal" students. Consequently, she suffered from great feelings of inferiority.

I have seen deaf children refuse to wear a hearing aid which would have made it possible for them to hear and learn in school. One second-grader refused to wear "that thing in my ear" because it made him feel foolish. He would remove it as soon as he left home each morning, even though he could hear very little in the classroom.

I know one little four-year-old boy whose glasses were lost at home. His family looked all over the house but couldn't find them. The child didn't seem to know where they were either. Finally he confessed, "Mommy, I have something to tell you."

She asked, "What?" and he replied, "I can find my glasses for you."

They went out in the backyard, and he retrieved them from a hole in the ground! This four-year-old had buried his glasses because they made him feel different! This is the discomfort felt by those who can't conform. They need our understanding and kindness.

A Boy Named Jeep Fenders

I was not always sensitive to the feelings of children who couldn't be like their peers. In fact, I had to learn to be kind to others during childhood. When I was nine years old, I attended a Sunday school class every week. One Sunday a new boy named Fred visited our class. I didn't stop to think that Fred might be uncomfortable as a stranger in our group, because I knew everyone and had many friends there. He sat quietly looking down at the floor. During the morning class I noticed that Fred had very strange ears. They were shaped in a kind of half-circle, like this: c . I remember thinking how much they looked like Jeep fenders. Have you ever seen the fenders on a Jeep, which go up and over the tires? Somehow I managed to see a resemblance to Fred's ears.

Then I did a very unkind thing. I told everyone that Fred had "Jeep-fender ears," and my friends thought that was terribly funny. They all laughed and began calling him "Jeep Fenders." Fred seemed to be accepting the joke pretty well. He sat with a little smile on his face (because he didn't know what to say), but it was hurting him deeply. Suddenly Fred stopped smiling. He exploded from his chair and hurried toward the door, crying. Then he ran out of the building and never came back to our church. I don't blame him. The way we acted was vicious, and I'm sure God was very displeased with me, especially.

However, the important thing to understand was how ignorant I was of Fred's feelings on that day. Believe it or not, I didn't really intend to hurt him. I had no idea that my joke made him feel terrible, and I was shocked when he ran from the classroom. I remember thinking about what I had done after he left, wishing I hadn't been so mean.

Why was I so cruel to Fred? It was because no one had ever told me that other people were as sensitive about being teased as I was. I thought I was the only one who didn't like to be laughed at. The teachers of my many Sunday school classes should have taught me to respect and protect the feelings of others. They should have helped me to be more Christlike.

That is why I'm writing these words to *you* today. I want you to know that others feel just like you do. They get the same lump in their throat when they're being teased, and they also cry when they're alone. You have *no business* making them feel worse than they already do, particularly someone who has a handicap or a strange body feature which makes him seem odd or strange. If a person's nose is too big, he already knows it, so don't talk about his nose. If he is too tall or short or fat or thin, don't make fun of him, don't give him a nickname, don't call attention to the feature he's already sensitive about, and don't give him any other reasons to feel bad. He has enough problems already.

The Daily Gloves

I'm reminded of a second-grader named Jeff whose teacher came to me a few years ago to help solve a riddle. She had noticed that Jeff always wore big, thick leather gloves to school every day. He was rarely seen without those gloves, even on the warmest days of the year. He obviously wasn't using them just to keep his hands warm. Of course his teacher would make him take them off when he came into the classroom, since he couldn't hold a pencil with the thickly padded fingers. But the moment Jeff went out to recess or lunch, he put on the gloves again.

Jeff's teacher just couldn't understand the reason for this behavior. Why was he so in love with those gloves? They weren't new or expensive; in fact, they were all scratched and dirty. But in talking to me about this problem, Jeff's teacher casually mentioned that he was the only black child in a classroom of white children. Then Jeff's behavior suddenly began to make sense. He was bothered by being different from his friends, as you and I would have been.

You see, when Jeff wore a long-sleeved shirt, trousers, shoes, and socks, *the only part of his skin that he could see was his hands.* By wearing those gloves, Jeff couldn't see his own black hands! His black skin certainly didn't make him inferior, but it made him feel unusual because he was the only non-white child in his room. He was embarrassed by this difference and tried to cover it up.

We need to understand friends like Jeff who feel inadequate and inferior. In fact, if we really love others as much as ourselves, we will give as much time and attention to helping them avoid pain and ridicule as we do ourselves. We will think about them as often as we think about ourselves. We will befriend the person who is a little different, or who is new at our school, or who is a foreign student with a strange accent, or who is in some kind of an embarrassing position. The Bible says that when you help that kind of needy person, it is as though you were doing it for Jesus Himself! *More than any other concept, this is the meaning of Christianity!*

God's View of Conformity

This brings us back to the principles of the Bible, which should guide our behavior in virtually every area of life. The Scriptures speak very plainly about the dangers of conformity. God in His wisdom knew that social pressure could keep us from doing what is right, and He spoke strongly against it.

Romans 12:2 warns, "Be not conformed to this world [in other words, don't let the world squeeze you into its mold], but be ye transformed [made into something new] by the renewing of your mind, that ye may prove what is that good and acceptable and perfect will of God." That is written in the King James Version of the Bible. Now let me read the same verse from *The Living Bible:* "Don't copy the behavior and the customs of this world, but be a new and different person, with a fresh newness in all you do and think. Then you will learn from your own experience how his ways will really satisfy you."

Another Scripture (First John 3:13) states it even more pointedly. It says, "My brothers, don't be surprised if the world hates you."

.. It is obvious from these verses (and many others) that God does not want us to follow the whims of the world around us. He expects us to say to ourselves, "I am going to control my behavior, my mind, my body, and my life. I will be like my friends in ways that don't matter, such as wearing fashionable clothes when convenient. But when it comes to being moral and obeying God and learning in school and keeping my body clean and healthy, then I won't let anybody tell me what to do. If they must laugh at me, then let them laugh. The joke won't be funny for very long. I'm not going to let *anything* keep me from living a Christian life. In other words, "I will not conform!"

The Courage of a Christian

I hope this discussion will help you to brace yourself against the pressures around you as an adolescent. And I also hope that you'll keep your pressure off other people (especially the handicapped) so they will be able to be happy and secure too. That will require Christian courage and confidence on your part.

I heard a true story of a young man who was a very courageous young Christian. After graduating from high school, he entered a state university near his home. During the first few weeks of class, a godless professor asked his class if any students considered themselves to be Christians. It was obvious that the professor intended to embarrass anyone who raised his hand. This young man looked around and saw that none of the two hundred students was going to admit his faith. What should he do? He either had to admit his Christianity or deny it, like Peter did when Jesus was about to be crucified. He suddenly held up his hand and said, "Yes, I'm a Christian."

The professor made him stand in front of the class and said, "How could you be so stupid to believe that God became a man and lived here on earth? That's ridiculous. Besides, I read the Bible and it didn't say a thing to me."

This young man looked right at the professor and said, "Sir, the Bible is God's letter to Christians. If you didn't understand it, that's what you get for reading somebody else's mail!"

Wasn't that a courageous answer? (That's the kind of reply I always think of later, when it's too late to say it.) Whether or not you can think up clever answers to disbelievers doesn't matter much. What *does* matter is that you protect your faith in God and be willing to be identified with Him.

As you get out of high school and into college, some people may try to make you feel foolish for trying to live a Christian life. When that happens I hope you'll remember our discussion about conformity, about group pressure, and about the commandment of God Himself: "Be not conformed."

3

`------------------------------------------`

Something Crazy Is
Happening To My Body

Let's turn our attention now to another new experience which will occur during the adolescent years. I'm sure you've noticed that adults are not just bigger than children, but their bodies are very different from those of boys and girls. They're shaped differently and they work differently. For those of you between ten and thirteen years of age, I want to discuss how your bodies will soon make this dramatic change from childhood to adulthood. Those of my readers who are teenagers will already have experienced some of the physical changes we'll be presenting.

The Big Boss Upstairs

The growing-up process is a wonderful and interesting event. It's all controlled by a tiny organ near the center of your brain called the *pituitary gland*.

This little organ is only the size of a small bean, yet it's called the master gland because it tells the rest of your glands what to do. It's the "big boss upstairs," and when it screams, your glandular system jumps. Somewhere within your own pituitary gland is a plan for your body. At just the right time, it will send out chemical messengers, called hormones, which will tell the rest of the glands in your body, "Get moving, it's time to grow up." In fact, those hormones will have many implications for your body during the next few years of your life.

There are several reasons why you ought to understand this aspect of physical development. First, if you don't know what is about to happen to your body, it can be pretty terrifying when everything goes crazy all at one time. It's not unusual for a teenager to begin worrying about himself. He wonders, "What's going on here? Do I have a disease? Could this be cancer? Is there something wrong with my body? Dare I discuss it with anybody?" These are unnecessary fears that result from ignorance or misinformation about the body. When young people understand the process, they know that these changes represent normal, natural events which they should have been anticipating. So I'm going to tell you exactly what you can expect in the period of early adolescence. There's just no reason for you to be anxious over these rapid physical changes.

Preparing for Parenthood

What can you expect to happen during early adolescence, and how will it all take place? The most important change that you will notice is that your body will begin to prepare itself for parenthood. Now I didn't say that you are about to become a parent (that should be years away), but that your body is about to *equip itself* with the ability to produce a child. That's one of the major changes that occurs during this period. The correct name for this time of sexual awakening is *puberty*. (Do you remember reading in the first chapter about driving your "car" through a little town by that name?)

A Boy's New Body

First let's discuss what happens to boys, and then we'll talk about girls. During puberty, a boy begins to grow very rapidly, faster than ever before in his life. His muscles will become much more like those of a man, and he'll get much stronger and better coordinated. That's why a junior high boy is usually a much better athlete than a fifth- or sixth-grader, and why a high school boy is a better athlete than a junior high boy. A dramatic increase occurs in his overall body size, strength, and coordination during this period.

Secondly, hair on a boy's body will begin to look more like the hair of a man. He'll notice the beginnings of a beard on his face, and he'll have to start shaving it every now and then. Hair will also grow under his arms for the first time, and also on what is called the pubic region (or what you may have called the private area), around his sex organs. The sex organs themselves will become larger and more like those of an adult male. These are evidences that the little boy is disappearing forever, and in his place will come a man, capable of becoming a father and taking care of his wife and family. This fantastic transformation reminds me in some ways of a caterpillar, which spins a cocoon around itself and then after awhile comes out as a totally different creature—a butterfly. Of course the changes in a boy are not that complete, but he will never be the same after undergoing this process of *maturation* (the medical word for growing up).

Rapid Changes

These rapid changes are just around the corner for many of you. The frightening thing for some kids is that they occur very suddenly, almost overnight. The pituitary gland quickly begins kicking everything into action. It barks its orders right and left, and your entire body seems to race around inside, trying to carry out these commands.

Everything is affected—even your voice will be different. I'm sure you've noticed how much lower your dad's voice is than your own. Have you ever wondered how it got that way? Was it always deep and gruff? Did it always sound like a foghorn? Can you imagine your dad in his crib as a baby saying "Goo, goo" in a deep voice? Of course not. He wasn't born that way. His voice changed during puberty, and that's what will happen to yours, too. However, an adolescent boy's voice is sometimes an embarrassment to him until this deepening process is finished, because it doesn't sound very solid. It squeaks and screeches and wobbles and cracks for a few months. But again, this is nothing to worry about, because the voice will soon be deep and steady. A little time is needed to complete this development of the vocal cords.

Solving Skin Problems

As I've stated, practically every part of your body is affected in one way or another by puberty. Even your skin will undergo major changes, whether you are a boy or a girl. In fact, this is probably the most distressing aspect of all the physical events that take place in early adolescence. One study of two thousand teenagers asked the question, "What do you most dislike about yourself?" Skin problems outranked every other reply by a wide margin.

Skin eruptions occur primarily as a result of an oily substance which is secreted during adolescence. The pores of the skin tend to fill up with this oil and become blocked. Since the oil can't escape, it hardens there and causes pimples or blackheads. You might expect to have these imperfections on your skin for several years, although some cases are milder than others.

When you get numerous pimples and blackheads regularly, the condition is called acne. If this happens, it will be very important for you to keep your skin clean, minimizing the oil and dirt on your face. It is also important to watch what you eat, since certain greasy foods are thought to contribute to the difficulty. If the problem is severe, you should ask your parents to take you to a *dermatologist,* who is a doctor specializing in skin problems. He will advise you on the best method of treatment.

Teenage Fatigue

Another physical problem occuring with both boys and girls during puberty is fatigue, or lack of energy. Your body will be investing so many of its resources into the growing process that it will seem to lack energy for other activities for a period of time. This phase usually doesn't last very long. However, this tired feeling is something you ought to anticipate. In fact, it should influence your behavior in two ways.

First, you must get plenty of sleep and rest during the period of rapid physical growth. That need is often not met, however, because teenagers feel that they should not have to go to bed as early as they did when they were a child. Therefore, they stay up too late and then drag through the next day in a state of exhaustion. Believe it or not, a twelve- or thirteen-year-old person actually needs more rest than when he was nine or ten, simply because of the acceleration in growth.

If your parents are also reading this book, I would suggest that they let you sleep on Saturday mornings if possible. It is often difficult for mothers and fathers to permit their overgrown son or daughter to lie in bed until 9:30 A.M. when the grass needs mowing. However, they should know that he is lying in bed because he needs more sleep, and they would be wise to let him get it. *Then* he can mow the lawn when he awakens, with a great smile of gratitude on his face!

Second, the foods you eat will also be very important during adolescence. Your body has to have the raw materials with which to construct those new muscle cells and bones and fibers that are in the plans. Hot dogs and donuts and milkshakes just won't do the job. It will be necessary for you to get a *balanced* diet during this time; it's even more important than when you were six or eight. If you don't eat right during this growth period, you will pay the price with sickness and various physical problems. Your body *must* have the vitamins and minerals and protein necessary to enlarge itself in so many ways.

The Beauty of Womanhood

Now let's talk about the many changes girls will experience during the years of puberty. A girl's body goes through even more complex changes than those of a boy, because it has to prepare itself for the very complicated task of motherhood. The way a woman's body functions to produce human life is one of the most beautiful mechanisms in all of God's universe. Let's look at that process for a moment.

All human life begins as one tiny cell, so small that you couldn't see it without a microscope. This first cell of life is called a zygote, which begins to divide and grow inside the mother's uterus.

The uterus is a special place inside the mother's lower abdomen, or what you may have called the stomach. Actually, it's not in the stomach at all, but below it. The uterus is a special little pouch that serves as a perfect environment for a growing and developing embryo. (An *embryo* is the name for a baby in its earliest stages of development.)

All the baby's needs for warmth and oxygen and nourishment are met constantly by the mother's body during the nine months before his birth. Any little slip-up during those very early days (the first three months especially), and the growing child will die. The embryo is extremely delicate, and the mother's body has to be in good physical condition in order to meet the requirements of the growing child.

In order to meet these requirements, a girl's body undergoes many changes during puberty. One of those important developments is called menstruation, which you've probably already heard about. This is a subject that girls will need to understand thoroughly in the days ahead. Most schools provide this information to girls in the fifth or sixth grade, so what I'll tell you now may just be a review of what you have seen and heard elsewhere. However, I feel it is important for boys to understand this process too, although they are seldom informed properly.

The Growing Life

When a woman becomes pregnant—that is, when the one-celled zygote is planted in her uterus after having a sexual relationship with a man, her body begins to protect this embryo and help it grow. It has to have oxygen and food and many chemicals which are necessary for life. The substances are delivered to the uterus automatically, through the mother's blood. But since the uterus has no way of knowing when a new life is going to be planted there, it must get ready to receive an embryo each month, just in case it happens. Therefore, blood accumulates on the walls of the uterus in order to nourish an embryo if the woman becomes pregnant. But if she *doesn't* become pregnant that month, then the uterine blood is not needed. It is released from the walls of the uterus and flows out through the vagina—that special opening through which babies are also born.

Every 28 days (this number varies a bit from person to person), a woman's body will get rid of this unnecessary blood which would have been used to nourish a baby if she had become pregnant. It usually takes about three to five days for the flow to stop, and during this time she wears a kind of cloth pad to absorb the blood. This process is called *menstruation*.

There are some very important attitudes that I want you to understand through this discussion. First, menstruation is not something for girls to dread and fear. Since the subject of blood causes us to shudder, some girls get very tense over this process happening to them. They start worrying about it and dreading its arrival, and some do not want it to happen at all. But actually, menstruation makes possible the most fantastic and exciting event that can ever occur—the creation of a new human being. What a miracle it is for a single cell, the zygote, to quietly split into two, then four, eight, and sixteen cells, and continue to divide until trillions of new cells are formed! A little heart slowly emerges within the cluster of cells, and begins beating to the rhythm of life. Then come fingers and toes and eyes and ears and all the internal organs. A special liquid (called amniotic fluid) surrounds the baby to protect him from any bumps or bruises the mother might receive. And there he stays for nine months, until he is capable of surviving in the world outside. Then at just the right moment the mother's body begins pushing the baby down the birth canal (the vagina) and into the waiting hands of the physician.

The Beauty of God's Design

The most beautiful aspect of this incredibly complicated system is that it all works *automatically* within a woman's body. It's almost as though the Master Designer, God Himself, were standing nearby, telling her what to do next. In fact, did you know that this is precisely what happens? We are told by King David, writing in the Psalms, that God is present during this creation of a new life. Let's read his description of that event (Psalm 139:13-15):

> You made all the delicate inner parts of my body, and knit them together in my mother's womb. Thank you for making me so wonderfully complex! It is amazing to think about. Your workmanship is marvelous—and how well I know it. You were there while I was being formed in utter seclusion!
> —*The Living Bible*

Not only did God supervise David's development in his mother's womb (another word for uterus), but He did the same thing for you and me! He has also scheduled each day of our lives and recorded every day in His book. That is the most reassuring thought that I've ever known!

So you see, menstruation is not an awful event for girls to dread. It is a signal that the body is preparing itself to cooperate with God in creating a new life, if that proves to be His will for a particular woman. Menstruation is the body's way of telling a girl that she is growing up . . . that she is not a child anymore . . . and that something very exciting is happening inside.

Know the Facts and Be at Peace

Now, girls, please don't worry about this aspect of your health. You will not bleed to death, I promise you. Menstruation is as natural as eating or sleeping or any other bodily process. If you feel you are abnormal in some way—if you're worried about some aspect of menstruation—if you think you're different or that maybe something has gone wrong—or if there's some pain associated with your menstruation or you have any question at all, then muster your courage and talk to your mother or your doctor or someone in whom you have confidence. In about 98 cases out of 100, the fears will prove to be unjustified. You will find that you are completely normal, and that the trouble was only in your lack of understanding of the mechanism.

Other Changes to Anticipate

Now, obviously, other things will begin to happen to your body at about the same time as menstruation. You will probably have a growth spurt just prior to your first menstruation. (Incidentally, the average age of first menstruation in American girls is now about twelve-and-one-half years of age, but it can occur as early as nine or ten years or as late as sixteen or seventeen. The age varies widely from girl to girl.)

During this time your body will become more rounded and curvy like your mother's. Your breasts will enlarge, and they may become sore occasionally (boys sometimes experience this soreness too). This doesn't mean that you have cancer or some other disease, but simply that your breasts are changing, like everything else in your body. Hair will also grow under your arms, on your legs, and in the pubic region, as with boys. These are the most obvious physical changes which take place, and when you see them happening you can kiss good-bye to childhood—it's full speed ahead toward adulthood!

The Bridge of Late Maturity

There's another important matter that I must discuss with boys and girls. Your road to adulthood not only passes over the canyon of inferiority, but it also crosses the shaky bridge of *late maturity*. What I'm talking about is the anxious feelings that occur when a person doesn't grow up as quickly as he expected, or as soon as his friends develop. These changes of puberty that I've been describing may occur as early as nine or ten years of age or as late as seventeen or eighteen, but *each boy and each girl has his or her own timetable*. Again, the age of development is supervised by the pituitary gland in the brain, which has everything under control. However, these individual timetables cause a lot of unnecessary worry among those who are either ahead of their friends or behind them. The age of puberty really doesn't have much meaning, but it can become a source of great worry and concern.

For example, let's suppose you're a thirteen-year-old girl whose body has not yet begun to change. You still look like Little Red Riding Hood; none of your adult features have begun to show up. As you look around at the other girls in your class, you notice that some of them already look like women. They're wearing bras, but you clearly don't need one.

Then you start worrying about what's occurring inside. "Is there something wrong with me? Why haven't these things happened to me yet?" Then you turn fourteen, and still nothing changes. Your body is just sitting there yawning at you, and you're really getting concerned. You lay awake at night wondering if you'll still look like a child when you're fifty years old. Your girlfriends are talking to each other about menstruation, but you can't share in the conversation because you know nothing about it. You feel different and odd, and you worry until you're almost sick with anxiety.

No Peach Fuzz

Or suppose you're a fifteen-year-old boy who has the same problem. You aren't nearly as strong as your friends, and since you haven't had your growth spurt, you're one of the shortest boys in your class. In fact, you're even shorter than most of the girls, because girls start their puberty growth before boys. The other boys are starting to shave, but you don't even have peach fuzz on your face. You pick up the telephone to talk to the operator, but your voice is so high that she thinks you're a girl. She says, "Yes, Ma'am." That may be the worst insult that's ever been thrown at you!

But the most painful thing of all is that the other guys have noticed that you're still a little boy, and they've begun to tease you. When you're in the locker room, they call you nicknames and make fun of the fact that you don't have pubic hair or that you're still short and scrawny.

What are you going to do if this happens in the next few years? Are you going to crack up? Will you grind your teeth and bite your nails and chew your tongue? I hope that won't be necessary in your life.

There's Nothing Wrong with You

Let me make a suggestion for those of you who grow up a little later than your friends. The main thing to remember is that *there's nothing wrong with you*. It's just as healthy to grow up later as earlier, and there's no reason to fear that you will never mature. Just hold steady for a year or two, and then the fireworks will all begin to pop for you, just as for everybody else! I can promise you that this is going to happen. If you don't believe me, take a look at all the adults around you. Do you see any of them that look like children? Of course not. *Everyone* grows up sooner or later.

Certainly it's never much fun to be laughed at by your friends, but if you know you'll be different for only a short time, maybe you can stand it. Most importantly, don't you be guilty of making another person feel bad about himself if you happen to grow before he does!

The Sex Appetite

As your body starts to change, you'll notice that you're beginning to be more interested in people of the opposite sex. Suddenly girls begin to look great to boys and the boys start appealing to the girls. How do I know this will happen? How can I predict it so accurately? Because sex will soon become an "appetite" within you. If you missed your breakfast this morning, I can predict that you'll be plenty hungry by two o'clock in the afternoon. Your body will ask for food. It's made that way. There are chemicals in your body that will make you feel hungry when you haven't eaten.

In the same way, some new chemicals in your body will begin to develop a brand-new appetite when you're between twelve and fifteen years old. This will not be a craving for food, but it will involve the matter called sex, or the male or female aspects of your nature. Every year as you get older, this appetite will become more and more a part of you. You'll want to spend more of your time with someone of the opposite sex. Eventually this desire may lead you to marriage. Marriage is a wonderful union for those who find the right person. However, let me offer a word of caution on that subject.

One of the biggest mistakes you can make with your life is to get married *too soon*. That can be tragic. I want to stress that point in your mind. For two people to get married before they are ready can be a disaster. Unfortunately, this happens all too frequently. I will say more about this subject later in the book, but I strongly advise you not to get married until you're at least twenty years of age. *Half of all teenage marriages* blow up within five years, causing many tears and problems. I don't want yours to be one of those broken homes.

Pretty Girls and Fascinating Boys

Now let me describe for you the feeling that sex will bring in the next few years. Boys will become very interested in the bodies of girls—in the way they're built, in their curves and softness, and in their pretty hair and eyes. Even their feminine feet may have an appeal to boys during this time. If you're a boy, it's very likely that you will think often about these fascinating creatures called girls, whom you used to hate so much! In fact, the sexual appetite is stronger in males between sixteen and eighteen years of age than at any other age in life.

Girls, on the other hand, will not be quite so excited over the shape and the look of a boy's body (although they will find them interesting). They will be more fascinated by the boy himself—the way he talks, the way he walks, the way he thinks. If you're a girl, you will probably get a "crush" on one boy after another. (A crush occurs when you begin to think that one particular person is absolutely fantastic, and you fantasize about the possibility of being married to that person. It is not uncommon to get a crush on a teacher or pastor or older man. Usually crushes are constantly changing, lasting only a few weeks or months before another one takes its place.)

Plain Talk About Sex

Now we need to talk very plainly about the subject of sexual intercourse. Remember what I told you at the beginning of this book. I'm going to be treating you like adults and withholding *no* subject that is relevant to you. Therefore, you must understand the importance of sexual relationships between a man and woman.

Sexual intercourse is the name given to the act that takes place when a man and a woman remove all their clothing (usually done in bed) and the man's sex organ (his *penis*) becomes very hard and straight. He puts his penis into the vagina of the woman while lying between her legs. They move around, in and out, until they both have a kind of tingly feeling which lasts for a minute or two. It's a very satisfying experience, which husbands and wives do regularly. You probably already know about sexual intercourse as I described it. But did you know that a man and woman do not have intercourse just to have babies? They do it to express love for each other and because they enjoy doing it. In this way they satisfy each other. They may have sexual intercourse two or three times a week, or maybe only once a month; each couple is different. But this is a fun part of marriage, and something that makes a husband and wife very special to each other. This is an act which they save just for each other.

God's Gift of Sex

This appetite for sex is something that God created within you. I want to make this point very strongly. Sex is not dirty and it is not evil. Nothing that God ever created could be dirty. The desire for sex was God's idea—not ours. He placed this part of our nature into us; He created those chemicals (hormones) that make the opposite sex appealing to us. He did this so we would want to have a family of our own. Without this desire there would be no marriage and no children and no love between a man and a woman. So sex is not a dirty thing at all; it's a wonderful, beautiful mechanism, no matter what you may have heard about it.

However, I must also tell you that God intends for us to control that desire for sexual intercourse. He has stated repeatedly in the Bible that we are to save our body for the person we will eventually marry, and that it is wrong to satisfy our appetite for sex with a boy or girl before we get married. There is just no other way to interpret the Biblical message. Some of your friends may tell you differently in the days ahead. You may hear Jack or Susie or Paul or Jane tell about how they explored each other's bodies. They'll tell you how exciting it was, and try to get you to do the same.

Decide Now

Let me state it more personally. It is very likely that *you* will have a chance to have sexual intercourse before you reach twenty years of age. Sooner or later that opportunity will come to you. You will be with a person of the opposite sex who will let you know that he or she will permit you to have this experience. You're going to have to decide between now and then what you'll do about that moment when it comes. You probably won't have time to think when it suddenly happens. My strongest advice is for you to decide *right now* to save your body for the one who will eventually be your marriage partner. If you don't control this desire you will later wish that you had.

Venereal Disease

God's commandment that we avoid sexual intercourse before marriage was not given in order to keep us from having pleasure. It was not His desire to take the fun out of life. To the contrary, it was actually His *love* that caused Him to forbid premarital intercourse, because so many harmful consequences occur when you refuse to obey Him.

You've probably heard about venereal disease, which is caused from having intercourse with someone who has caught it from another carrier. Syphilis, gonorrhea, and other diseases are very widespread today. Our country is having an epidemic of these diseases, and they have a damaging effect on the body if they go untreated. But there are other consequences for those who have premarital sex. They run the risk of bringing an unwanted baby into the world by this act. When that occurs, they face the responsibility of raising a human being—a little life with all its needs for love and discipline and the stability of a home—but they have no way to take care of him or meet his needs. That is tragic.

The Sin of Impurity

But just as serious are the changes that take place within a person's *mind* when he has intercourse outside the bonds of marriage. First, and most important, his relationship with God is sacrificed. Premarital sex is a sin, and a person just can't be friends with God if he is going to continue to sin deliberately and willfully. First John 1:6 says, "If we say we are His friends but go on living in spiritual darkness and sin, we are lying" *(The Living Bible)*. It's as simple as that. Furthermore, nothing can be hidden from God, as you know, because He sees everything.

Sin always has a destructive effect on a young person. But I believe the sin of premarital sex is especially damaging to the person who engages in it. He or she loses the innocence of youth, and sometimes becomes hard and cold as a person. It's also likely to affect his or her later marriage, because that special experience which should have been shared with just one person is not so special anymore. More than one person has had a sample of it.

So you see, there are many obvious reasons why God has told us to control our sexual desires. What I'm saying is that God has commanded us not to have sex before marriage in order to spare us these many other effects of this sin. In fact, the *worst* consequence is one I have not yet mentioned, relating to the judgment of God in the life to come. We are told very clearly in the Bible that our lives will be laid bare before Him, and He will know every secret. Our eternal destinies actually depend on our faith in God and our obedience to Him.

Self-Stimulation

Let me talk with you now about a related subject called masturbation. This is something you may have heard about from your friends. If not, you will hear it soon. Masturbation is the act of rubbing your own sex organs in order to get that same tingly feeling that you would have if you were participating in intercourse. Most boys do this at some time during adolescence, and so do many girls.

Many rumors surround this act—scary stories about what happens to people who do it. Some people say that masturbating will make you go crazy. Others say it will keep you from being able to have a child later on. Still others say it will make you weak and sickly. You may hear all kinds of drastic warnings about the consequences of masturbating. Well, I can tell you right now that not one of these stories is true.

They are all falsehoods. If masturbation made people go crazy, there would be a lot more crazy people in the world than there are!

Still, the subject of masturbation is a very controversial one. Christian people have different opinions about how God views this act. Unfortunately, I can't speak directly for God on this subject, since His Holy Word, the Bible, is silent at this point. I will tell you what I *believe*, although I certainly do not want to contradict what your parents or your pastor believe. It is my *opinion* that masturbation is not much of an issue with God. It's a normal part of adolescence which involves no one else. It does not cause disease, it does not produce babies, and Jesus did not mention it in the Bible. I'm not telling you to masturbate, and I hope you won't feel the need for it. But if you do, it is my opinion that you should not struggle with guilt over it.

Why do I tell you this? Because I deal with so many Christian young people who are torn apart with guilt over masturbation; they want to stop and just can't. I would like to help you avoid that agony. The best I can do is suggest that you talk with God personally about this matter and decide what He wants you to do. I'll leave it there between you and Him.

Nocturnal Emissions

One other thing that bothers boys during adolescence is the occurrence of "wet dreams." Doctors call these *nocturnal emissions*. This refers to the fluid which comes out of a boy's penis occasionally at night. The fluid is called semen, and contains millions of cells so tiny that you can't even see them. One of these cells could become a child if it were injected into a female and combined with her egg cell. (That would compose the zygote which we discussed earlier.) This semen sometimes is released during a nighttime dream; then the boy finds the stain on his pajamas the next morning and begins to worry about what is going on. However, this event is perfectly normal. It happens to almost all boys, and is nothing to worry about. A nocturnal emission is just his body's way of getting rid of the extra fluid that has accumulated.

The Questions of Fear

Have you noticed how many times I've said in this chapter, "It's nothing to be concerned about; it's normal; don't worry"? The reason behind my reassurances is this: most young people become frightened about their own sexual development. As I stated in my book *Dare to Discipline*, teenagers often worry about the following kinds of questions during the early part of puberty.

1. Are all these changes supposed to be happening?

2. Is there something wrong with me?

3. Do I have a disease or an abnormality?

4. Am I going to be different from other people?

5. Does this pain in my breast mean I have cancer? (Remember, I mentioned that the breasts sometimes get sore during adolescence.)

6. Will I be able to have intercourse, or will there be something wrong with me?

7. Will the boys laugh at me? Will the girls reject me? (It's very common for people to feel they're not going to be attractive to the opposite sex and that nobody will want them because they are not as pretty or handsome as they wish they could be.)

8. Will God punish me for the sexual thoughts that I have? (I told you that you're likely to think about the opposite sex often during these years. When this happens you may feel guilty for the thoughts that occur.)

9. Wouldn't it be awful if I became a homosexual? (A homosexual is someone who is not attracted

to the opposite sex, but who is attracted to the *same* sex. It's a boy's interest in boys or a girl's interest in girls. Homosexuality is an abnormal desire that reflects deep problems, but it doesn't happen very often and it's not likely to happen to you.)

10. Could I get pregnant without having sexual relations? (This is another possibility that some young girls fear—that they could find themselves pregnant even if they haven't had sexual relations. I want you to know that this *never* happens; it's an impossibility. Only one time in all of history did this occur, and that's when the virgin Mary, Jesus' mother, became pregnant even though she had never had sexual intercourse. Jesus was conceived or planted in her uterus by God Himself. That's the only time in the world's history that a human being has ever been born without the father doing his part by providing half of the cell that becomes the zygote.)

11. Do some people fail to mature sexually? (Any system of the body can malfunction, but this one *rarely* fails.)

12. Will my modesty be sacrificed? (It's common during the early adolescent years for you to become extremely modest about your body. You know it's changing and you don't want anybody to see it. Therefore, you may worry about being in a doctor's office and having to take off your clothes in front of other people.)

No Need to Fear

Let me say it one more time: these kinds of fears are almost universal during the early years of adolescence. Nearly everyone growing up in our culture worries and frets over the subject of sex. I want to help you avoid those anxieties. Your sexual development is a normal event that is being controlled inside your body. It will work out all right, so you can just relax and let it happen. However, you will have to control your sexual desires in the years ahead, and that will require determination and will power. But if you can learn to channel your sexual impulses the way God intended, this part of your nature can be one of the most fascinating and wonderful aspects of your life, perhaps contributing to a successful and happy marriage in the years ahead.

4

I Think I've Fallen
In Love

Today it is very common to hear someone talking
about "falling in love" with another person. But have
you ever stopped to ask yourself what these words actually mean? What changes take place in the minds of
men and women who have fallen in love? How can
they know when that love is genuine? Can they be
fooled, thinking they are "in love" when they aren't?
What is necessary to keep their love alive?

Can you answer these questions about the meaning of love? Most young people cannot. In fact, there
is great confusion among teenagers about this important subject. It is my belief that the high divorce rate
in our country results, in part, from the failure of newly-
weds to understand what love is, what it is not, and
how to make sense out of their emotions.

This subject of romantic love may not be very interesting to you now. You might even think it is rather
silly. However, unless you are a very unusual person,

you are likely to become extremely attracted to members of the opposite sex in the years immediately ahead. And as you get older, the possibility of marriage will present itself. Girls usually start thinking about marriage several years before boys do, but sooner or later young men begin to "dig" the same idea. That's when some fascinating events start to unfold.

The Ecstasy of Love

Most people in their early twenties (or before) begin searching for the perfect human being with whom to spend the rest of their lives. And when they find someone who seems to fit that general description, they tumble head over heels into sheer ecstasy. There is no feeling in the world quite like it. They can hardly take their eyes off each other and they want to be together every moment of the day. They spend their hours picnicking in parks and walking in the rain and sitting glassy-eyed by a crackling fire. They even invade one another's dreams at night. Believe me when I say "falling in love" is a thrilling experience. I know—I've done it hundreds of times!

This exhilaration of romantic love is so captivating that it leads naturally to the question of marriage. A starry-eyed couple seems to reason, "If this feeling is so neat, why don't we spend our entire lives together?" So they begin making plans for a wedding. They set the date and call the preacher and order the flowers. Finally the big night arrives with the bride nervous and the groom bewildered. The bride's mother cries through the ceremony and her father is pale and tense. The bratty little flower girl refuses to walk down the aisle, and the groom's sister butchers a sentimental song about eternal love. But somehow the couple says, "I do," and the preacher pronounces them "man and wife." Then they march down the aisle, each flashing 32 teeth, as they head for the reception room.

There is noise and laughter and kisses for the bride as the people file by to offer best wishes to the new Mr. and Mrs. They eat the nuts and choke down the cake and talk about their own weddings. At last the bride and groom run from the church in a shower of rice and confetti, and drive off to start a new life. As they leave, they hear the groom's sister crooning, "They've only just begun. . . ."

So far, so good. Everyone seems happy and excited. But for this grinning young couple, serious trouble lies ahead. Almost from the first day of the honeymoon, something changes in their relationship. That tremendous excitement and enthusiasm begins to fade a bit. Marriage itself takes on a new look. Instead of being something they hoped they could capture if they were lucky, it now becomes a lifetime entanglement that has sprung a trap in reverse. They wonder silently whether this is what they really wanted, or whether they've made a hasty decision. The awful thought occurs that they might have stumbled into the biggest mistake of their lives.

Scratching and Clawing

The third day of the honeymoon brings the first real fight. The couple disagreed on where they should eat dinner and how much money they should spend. She wanted to eat at a romantic restaurant, and he thought they should have a hamburger at Ronald McDonald's. It was a minor argument, but some harsh words were exchanged that further damaged the romantic feeling with which they began. They would learn to hurt each other more effectively in the months ahead.

They had only been home from the honeymoon about a week when the first all-out battle occurred. Insults were hurled back and forth like nuclear warheads. Deep feelings of hurt and resentment then raged on both sides, followed by long periods of icy silence. The husband left home for two hours and his wife called her mother. From then to the bitter end, we see two extremely bitter and unhappy people who cry themselves to sleep at night. And what is worse, they may have produced another member of the family by that time . . . a toothless little guy who has to have his diapers changed every 45 minutes. This toddler will grow up in a broken home and will never fully understand "why daddy doesn't live here anymore."

The Tragedy of Divorce

Now obviously this pessimistic description of marriage isn't accurate in *all* cases, but it does happen far too often. The divorce rate in the United States is higher than that of any other civilized nation in the world. In fact, it is known that *50 percent* of all teenage marriages end in divorce *within the first five years!* What a tragically high percentage! It means that *half* of all the people who thought they were "in love"—those who were tremendously excited with each other—quickly become disillusioned, bitter, unhappy, and broken. And we must ask ourselves, "Why?" Why is this happening? How do all these people get misled? What caused the flame of love to flicker and go out? How did their mutual affection turn into such hatred and anger and conflict just a few months later? These questions are extremely important to *you*, if a similar disaster is to be avoided in your own life. To answer them, we must examine the meaning of romantic love more closely.

Beliefs About Love

We'll begin our study by measuring how well you already understand this concept of marital love. I have developed a short quiz to sample your knowledge and beliefs on this important topic. May I suggest that you take a sheet of paper and number it from 1 to 10. Then answer the following questions, True or False.

_____ 1. I believe that "love at first sight" occurs between some people.

_____ 2. I believe that it's easy to distinguish real love from infatuation.

_____ 3. I believe that people who sincerely love each other will not fight and argue.

_____ 4. I believe that God selects one particular person for each of us to marry, and that He will guide us together.

_____ 5. I believe that if a man and woman genuinely love each other, then hardships and troubles will have little or no effect on their relationship.

_____ 6. I believe that it's better to marry the wrong person than to remain single and lonely throughout life.

_____ 7. I believe that it's not harmful or sinful to have sexual intercourse before marriage if the couple has a meaningful relationship.

_____ 8. I believe that if a couple is genuinely in love, that condition is permanent and will last a lifetime.

_____ 9. I believe that short courtships, six months or less, are best.

_____ 10. I believe that teenagers are more capable of genuine love than are older people.

Answers to the Questions

The quiz you have just taken is not intended to be a highly scientific test. In fact, some people might even have different opinions about the correct answers to each item. However, let me give you my views regarding the ten questions and the explanations behind them

Instant Love?

Question Number 1: "I believe that love at first sight occurs between some people."

There are individuals who believe that romantic love occasionally hits two strangers like a bolt of lightning the moment they first see each other. There they are, just walking down the sidewalk or sitting in church, and Zappo! Their eyes pop, their ears ring, their toes curl, and they have "fallen in love."

I hate to sound unromantic, but that kind of instant love is an *impossibility*. You can't love someone whom you do not know, someone who is a total stranger. I can't deny that some very strong feelings may occur the first time you see a particular member of the opposite sex. He is handsome (or she is pretty) and you like his eyes and the sound of his voice and the confidence he displays. Everything about him is appealing, and you feel a powerful attraction toward this new dreamboat. You may think, therefore, that you have fallen in love with him from the first moment you were together. But in reality, you have fallen in love with his *image*—you don't even know the real person. You're not acquainted with his thoughts, habits, hopes, fears, plans, skills, abilities, or manners. So you can't say you love that *total* person when you've only met his outer shell.

Confusion in Music

Many teen songs show that the writers did not know the difference between genuine love and the temporary feelings described above. One popular song, for example, contained this phrase: "Before the dance was through, I knew I was in luv with yew." Come on now, that's not love! During the course of the dance this young fellow merely had a few warm thoughts and figured he had somehow slid into romance during the second stanza! But beware: *any feeling that arrives during one dance might just disappear during the next.*

Another songwriter penned these words: "I didn't know just what to do, so I whispered 'I love you.'" Now isn't that weird? The idea of making a lifetime commitment on the basis of confusion seems kind of silly to me! Yet that is what often happens. There's an awkward moment between a boy and a girl, and he isn't sure of himself, so he says, "I love you." His girl-friend gets shook up and thinks, "Fantastic! This guy's falling in love with me!" So she returns the compliment, and they hustle down the road toward disaster.

The Partridge Family recorded a song which stated, "I woke up in love this day, went to sleep with you on my mind." There's the error again. The singer had fallen in love sometime during the night. Isn't that sweet? Don't you see how this kind of love is *nothing more than a frame of mind?* It came over-night, and it can leave overnight.

There are dozens of examples showing confusion about love in today's teen music. However, the song that gets my vote for having the dumbest lyrics of the century was popular during the sixties. It was sung by a rock group named "The Doors." They recorded a number entitled "Hello, I love you, won't you tell me your name?" Will someone explain how you can love a person about whom you know absolutely nothing? What nonsense!

"How Can It Be Wrong When It Feels So Right?"

Let me repeat that the *feeling* of romantic excitement can occur instantly between a man and woman, as it did for those writing the songs mentioned above. Furthermore, those feelings can sometimes gradually lead to genuine love upon which a successful marriage can be based. In most cases, however, this momentary enthusiasm will be stone-cold-dead in twelve months. That's why it's so dangerous to make any lifelong decisions on the basis of any temporary emotion.

Debbie Boone once recorded an immensely popular song entitled, "You Light Up My Life." In it was the phrase, "It can't be wrong when it feels so right." Unfortunately, I could show her many bitter divorced people who once felt marvelous about the relationship which now haunts them. Some of them were fooled by "love at first sight."

Real Love or Infatuation?

Question Number 2: "I believe that it's easy to distinguish real love from infatuation."

I hope you marked this item "false," because it is definitely not accurate. The emotional explosion which occurs during infatuation makes it difficult to think clearly about *anything*. It is one of the most exhilarating events in human experience, being more fantastic than a roller coaster ride or a trip to Disneyland! Someday you will know what I mean. When it happens to you, however, there are two important facts about infatuation which you should remember.

First, "puppy love" or infatuation is highly *self-centered*. Let me explain by offering an illustration.

When I was in college a number of years ago, my parents traveled throughout the year. Therefore, I had no place to go when school was not in session. During the summer months, especially, I had to stay in the school dormitory while the other students went home to visit their parents. I usually got a job nearby and would return from work each evening to my quiet, boring room. A couple of other guys also stayed in the dormitory, but I didn't know either of them very well. Consequently, I usually spent a very lonely summer during those college days.

As you can imagine, I would begin to get excited near the end of August each year, anticipating the return of my friends in September. Finally they would arrive, and the old dormitory would again rock with laughter and noise and fun. Those were great days. But I was even more anxious for the *girls* to return to school. I hadn't had a date since May, and I couldn't wait for the "crop" of young ladies to show up for classes. Therefore, I was ripe for love every autumn. I would fall hopelessly in love with someone . . . anyone . . . on September 12th of each year. There was no question about it happening—the same thing occurred four years in a row. Each September my world would suddenly turn upside down: I couldn't sleep, I couldn't eat, and I couldn't study. (In fact, studying was one of the first things to go!) It was a truly thrilling event, as predictable as Thanksgiving or Christmas.

Don't you see how self-centered my "love" was each September? I would tell my friends, "*I* can't believe how fantastic this is. *I* never felt this way before. This is the greatest thing that ever happened to *me*." There can be little doubt about it—I had not fallen in love with a girl, but I had fallen in love with *love!* The young lady for whom I had "gone bananas" was merely a prize to be won . . . an object to be captured. She was usually forgotten and replaced by the following January.

Genuine love is very different from this temporary infatuation. Instead, it is focused on another human being. It brings a deep desire to make that person happy . . . to meet their needs and satisfy their desires and protect their interests. Real love is best described as being unselfish in all aspects, even if a personal sacrifice is required in the relationship.

Short-Lived Infatuation

The second fact about infatuation which you should know is that it *never* lasts very long. If there is one message in this chapter which is more important than all the others, this is it! Let me repeat it: that exciting feeling between two new "lovers" *never* continues for life. It can't last, simply because human emotions are constantly changing. Even when people *genuinely* love each other, there are times of great closeness, times when they feel nothing for each other, and times when they are irritable and grumpy. Emotions are like that, swinging regularly from high to low to high to low. (We'll return to this point later.) Therefore, it is *impossible* for a married couple to maintain that peak of intensity with which their relationship began.

Why is it so important to understand the temporary nature of early romantic love? Because some young people plunge quickly into marriage, before their emotions have even taken the first dip into apathy. They're still in the first "fever" on the wedding day. Unfortunately, however, they receive a great shock during the months (or days) that follow when they awaken one morning without that exciting feeling down inside. It is wise to understand that the "fever" of love can easily turn into a rash in the months that follow.

Surprisingly, each of the sad young couples who eventually stand before a judge in the divorce courts thoroughly believed themselves to be "in love" at the beginning. They didn't always hate the person they married. There was a time when their happiness seemed to be above any hardship or difficulty. But their good feelings disappeared like snow on a warm day, melting and running toward the gutter.

What's the Difference?

Even for those who know that infatuation is self-centered and temporary, they may eventually confuse it with genuine love. How, then, can they tell the difference between these two "conditions?" How can they interpret their own feelings? How can they avoid making a disastrous mistake?

To my knowledge, there is only *one* way to distinguish puppy love from the real thing: give yourself time to test your emotions. You will gradually come to understand your own mind and know what is best for the other person. How long will this process take? It differs from person to person, but in general, the younger you are, the longer you should wait. As I stated earlier, it is my opinion that teenagers should not get married until they reach their twenties, and only then if they have been sweethearts for at least two years. This recommendation is not offered for my purposes or to impose parental wishes on teenagers. Rather, it is suggested to help prevent some of the painful divorces which bring deep wounds to so many young people today.

No Arguments?

Question Number 3: "I believe that people who sincerely love each other will not fight and argue."

The answer to this third item may surprise you. (In fact, the average person misses at least three or four of these ten questions about love.) The statement above is false. People who genuinely love each other still have differences of opinion. They still disagree. They still become irritable. They still fight and argue on occasion.

Let me describe a common scene which brings conflict between a loving husband and wife. The father drives home from a bad day at the office. He parks his car in the driveway and walks wearily into the house. His wife meets him at the door, and she is equally tired. The children have been wearing on her nerves all day. She tells her husband that the washing machine is broken and there is water all over the floor and everything has gone wrong. On their desk is a big stack of bills that the family is unable to pay. Both the mother and father are on edge and grumpy. Under these circumstances it's very easy for people who actually love each other to find themselves arguing and fighting. Besides, there are honest differences of opinion about important subjects. They may disagree about how to spend their money, where to go to church, and many other issues that divide them. But even in the midst of these struggles it is still possible for them to love each other very deeply.

Let me state it more strongly. I have seen very few marriages which are so harmonious and stable that the husband and wife never have this kind of disagreement. You can expect some conflict in your own marriage even though you are deeply in love with your mate. More specifically, I would predict that the first year of marriage will be the most difficult twelve months of your first decade together. It will be a time of adjustment; you'll have to decide how your marriage is going to function and who will spend your money and where you'll go on vacations. These issues may heat your emotions and set off some pretty serious conflicts in your home.

Work on Your Differences

If this occurs, don't think your marriage is doomed, or that you've necessarily made a big mistake. What it means is that both of you must compromise and seek solutions to your problems. That's the difference between a good marriage and a bad one. Both have moments of struggle, but in a healthy relationship the husband and wife search for answers and areas of agreement because they love each other very much.

What, then, is a "bad" marriage? It is one where each partner loves himself more than the other person, where these attitudes lurk in the mind: "I married you because I thought you would be good for me," or, "I married you because I wanted someone to help me take care of my home," or, "I married you because I hoped you would earn a lot of money for me." You see, when marriage occurs for selfish reasons, then the routine arguments become more serious. They no longer reflect differences of opinion, but become fights to the death. Each person then tries to hurt the other person, who has become a bitter enemy.

Dreams of Marriage

Question Number 4: "I believe that God selects one particular person for each of us to marry, and that He will guide us together."

I have great faith in God, and I believe that all of the important decisions of life should be preceded by prayer and requests for divine guidance. Our heavenly Father, in response, is very loving and merciful to those who seek His help; He will reveal His wishes and influence on all important decisions. Nevertheless, the answer to Question Number 4 is "false." In fact, those who believe that God automatically puts the right people together are in danger of making a tragic error in judgment. They may think the first person with whom they are infatuated is the lover sent by the Lord, and off they tear into forty years of conflict.

I'll never forget the unhappy fellow who told me he was awakened by a powerful dream in the middle of the night. It seemed to say, "Go marry Susan." Ralph had not been praying for God's leadership, yet he thought this order came directly from the Lord. The next day he called Susan (whom he had dated only two or three times) and said, "God told me to marry you!" Susan felt she shouldn't argue with the Almighty, and she accepted. Their marriage has been most unhappy and unfortunate, appearing to be a mistake from a human point of view. Neither partner now believes that God actually spoke to Ralph in the middle of the night, but that his *own* impression fooled him.

Let me stress that it is *extremely* important for you to choose your marriage partner very carefully. The Lord has given you good judgment, and He expects you to use it in making the decisions of life. It is possible, in my opinion, to love Jesus and be a good Christian, yet make a hasty decision to marry the wrong person. God doesn't sit in heaven with a list of names, saying, "Let's see. I'll take Jack and put him with Nancy." In other words, our heavenly Father does not operate a routine matchmaking service for those who call themselves by His name!

Before you settle on a plan to be married, I suggest that you take the matter to the Lord in prayer. Ask Him to guide your paths in this vitally important decision. I'm sure He'll answer that request. But this kind of prayer is similar to one in which you are asking God to heal a disease. Just because you are a Christian doesn't mean you'll never get sick. God can heal that disorder if you ask Him (and if it is His will to do so), but *He isn't obligated* to help you if you don't ask Him.

Happy Hardships?

Question Number 5: "I believe that if a man and a woman genuinely love each other, then hardships and troubles will have little or no effect on their relationship."

Again, the answer is "false." Love is like life—it is delicate and fragile. It can be broken and crushed and ruined. The death of a family member, or sickness, or poverty can severely damage a genuine loving relationship.

I'm on the staff of a children's hospital, where some very tragic events occur every day. I see little children in great pain and sickness. I see boys and girls who have cancer and heart trouble and various deformities. Some are in the process of dying, others have brains that don't work properly, and still others have been born with strange physical malfunctions. These problems often make their parents feel guilty, even though they are not to blame for the sicknesses. Sometimes the guilt of having a diseased child is so damaging that a home can actually be destroyed by it. This is only one example of how a love relationship can be affected by one's circumstances and environment.

Someone said, "Love conquers all." That is not always true. It is important to know that you have to work to keep love alive; you have to protect it and maintain it, just like you would a delicate flower. This point is so important that I want to come back to it in a moment.

Wait If You Have To

Question Number 6: "I believe it's better to marry the wrong person than to remain single and lonely throughout life."

Once more, the correct answer is "false." I think it is much better to still be looking for the right person than to be involved in a bad marriage, even though being single may mean being lonely.

It is a wonderful blessing for a man and woman to be happily married, enjoying each other's friendship and perhaps raising a child or two. However, God did not intend for everyone to fit this pattern. The Apostle Paul even said that it is better for some people not to get married, especially those who are called to carry heavy responsibility in Christian work. Therefore, it is unwise to seek marriage at any cost.

People who fear they won't be able to get married are sometimes willing to accept any invitation that is offered, even if it comes from someone they don't love. That can be tragic. It is far better to remain single than to spend your lifetime scratching and clawing and fighting with a mate when you should never have married in the first place.

Sex Before Marriage?

Question Number 7: "I believe that it's not harmful or sinful to have sexual intercourse before marriage if the couple has a meaningful relationship."

I certainly hope you know by now that the above statement is absolutely false. Nevertheless, many people in our society have decided that the old rules no longer apply. "Everything has changed," they say; "now there's a new morality. There's nothing wrong with having sexual relations—with exploring the body of a person of the opposite sex—provided both of you seem to like each other." This is the most dangerous of all of the mistaken ideas about love, because it has many terrible consequences.

God's view of sex outside marriage is abundantly clear. If you are a Christian and if you believe that the Bible is the guide for your daily life, there can be no doubt about what is right and what is wrong. Let me read to you directly from *The Living Bible*:

> Honor your marriage and its vows, and be pure. [Marriage is a promise to be faithful to one person throughout life. God expects us to honor that commitment, not only after marriage, but before.] For God will surely punish all those who are immoral or commit adultery (Hebrews 13:4).

This same message appears repeatedly throughout the Bible, and it is obviously what God wants for our lives. Consider the following advice offered by King Solomon, one of the most brilliant men who ever lived:

> I was looking out the window of my house one day, and saw a simple-minded lad, a young man lacking common sense, walking at twilight down the street to the house of this wayward girl, a prostitute. She approached him, saucy and pert, and dressed seductively. She was the brash, coarse type, seen often in the streets and markets, soliciting at every corner for men to be her lovers.
>
> She put her arms around him and kissed him, and with a saucy look she said, "I've decided to forget our quarrel! I was just coming to look for you, and here you are! My bed is spread with lovely colored sheets of finest linen imported from Egypt, perfumed with myrrh, aloes and cinnamon. Come on, let's take our fill of love until morning, for my husband is away on a long trip. He has taken a wallet full of money with him, and won't return for several days."
>
> So she seduced him with her pretty speech, her coaxing and wheedling, until he yielded to her. He

couldn't resist her flattery. He followed her as an ox going to the butcher, or as a stag that is trapped, waiting to be killed with an arrow through its heart. He was as a bird flying into a snare, not knowing the fate awaiting it there.

Listen to me, young men, and not only listen but obey; don't let your desires get out of hand; don't let yourself think about her. Don't go near her; stay away from where she walks, lest she tempt you and seduce you. For she has been the ruin of multitudes— a vast host of men have been her victims. If you want to find the road to hell, look for her house (Proverbs 7:6-27 TLB).

Although it appears that Solomon was just warning *men* not to be immoral, that is not true. The laws of God apply equally to men and women, and they are designed for our benefit. The Lord has not given us meaningless restrictions in order to interfere with our fun and happiness. Rather, He has warned us against certain behaviors that will be harmful to ourselves and to the people living around us. Just today I read this verse from the 19th Psalm:

God's laws are perfect. They protect us, make us wise, and give us joy and light. . . . They warn us away from harm and give success to those who obey them (Psalm 19:7, 8, 11 TLB).

Don't believe those ungodly people who tell you that the "old rules" are out of date. God's instructions will *never* be out of date, and we would be wise to heed them in every aspect of our lives.

Let me share one more Scripture with you which lists those timeless instructions from the Lord:

Away then with sinful, earthly things; deaden the evil desires lurking within you; have nothing to do with sexual sin, impurity, lust and shameful desires; don't worship the good things of life, for that is idolatry. God's terrible anger is upon those who do such things. You used to do them when your life was still part of this world; but now is the time to cast off and throw away all these rotten garments of anger, hatred, cursing, and dirty language.

Don't tell lies to each other; it was your old life with all its wickedness that did that sort of thing; now it is dead and gone. You are living a brand new kind of life that is continually learning more and more of what is right, and trying constantly to be more and more like Christ, who created this new life within you. In this new life one's nationality or race or education or social position is unimportant; such things mean nothing. Whether a person has Christ is what matters, and he is equally available to all.

Since you have been chosen by God who has given you this new kind of life, and because of his deep love and concern for you, you should practice tender-hearted mercy and kindness to others. Don't worry about making a good impression on them but be ready to suffer quietly and patiently. Be gentle and ready to forgive; never hold grudges. Remember, the Lord forgave you, so you must forgive others.

Most of all, let love guide your life, for then the whole church will stay together in perfect harmony (Colossians 3:5-14 TLB).

Love Forever?

Question Number 8: "I believe that if a couple is genuinely in love, that condition is permanent and will last a lifetime."

I answered this question within Item 5, and it is also "false." I told you that love has to be maintained or it can die. This is probably the most important of the ten items for those who are already married. Even your parents should be aware that their love can die if they don't work to keep it alive. They should take time to be together, to talk to each other and to pray together. They should not permit anything to damage or weaken their relationship. Love must be supported and fed and protected, just like a little infant that is growing up at home. I hope you will remember this point when (and if) you have a marriage of your own.

Short Courtships?

Question Number 9: "I believe that short court-ships, six months or less, are best."

This issue was discussed within the response to the second question, but we'll repeat the message briefly. To the surprise of no one by this point, the correct answer again is false. You must give yourself time to know your own feelings, to let them rise and fall naturally, before they can be interpreted properly. And as I've stated, it is extremely dangerous to lock yourself into a permanent relationship before you even have a chance to become acquainted with your mind or to determine what you want out of life. I've seen many short courtships that produced equally short marriages, and I hope yours will not be one of them.

Young and Old Lovers

Question Number 10: "I believe that teenagers are more capable of genuine love than are older people."

The answer to this final item is also "false," because genuine love requires a certain measure of maturity. You see, dedicated love is only possible for those who have the ability to give of themselves. Love is not grabbing, or self-centered, or selfish. Real love is being able to contribute to the happiness of another person without expecting to get anything in return. And that unselfishness demands considerable maturity, which rarely occurs during the tumultuous years of adolescence. That's why teenage marriages often begin to collapse shortly after the honeymoon.

The Frying Pan and the Fire

Let me offer one further word of advice about early marriages. By all means don't make the mistake of using marriage as a way of getting away from your parents or your present circumstances. Some seventeen- or eighteen-year-old men and women become tired of their homes, like the girl who told me the only time she gets homesick is when she is at home. They don't communicate with their parents, and they fight with their brothers and sisters. Then at a moment of great unhappiness, along comes a chance to set up housekeeping with someone else who is equally miserable at home. Getting married may seem like an easy solution to two major problems, but it rarely works that way. That's just like jumping from the frying pan into the fire. Such a union can be (and usually is) a disastrous relationship. Of all the reasons for entering into marriage, the desire to escape from mom or dad is one of the worst.

In summary, I'll repeat the suggestion offered earlier: choose your mate very carefully *after your twentieth birthday*. That free advice could prevent a lifetime of grief for you and another person.

The Real Meaning of Love

Now that you've read the answers to the ten items on the test, you know that they are all false statements. The reason I chose them is because they represent the ten most common misconceptions about the meaning of love. These are the ten mistaken ideas that I hear most often when counseling with young people.

Let me summarize the message of this chapter by giving a very personal illustration. When my wife, Shirley, was seven years old, she had a very sad home situation involving an alcoholic father. That caused her to think about the person she would marry someday. More than anything else in the world, she wanted to grow up and have a happy home with a Christian husband. God saw this inconspicuous little girl go into her bedroom and shut the door. He saw her get on her knees and begin to pray in her childlike manner that God would bless her future home and give her a husband who would love and care for her. God answered that prayer. Shirley and I now have a beautiful marriage and have been blessed with two children who mean everything to us.

I met Shirley when we were in college (during September, of course) and *gradually* came to love her. Notice that I didn't say that I "fell in love" with her. That phrase is misleading, making young people believe that falling in love is like tumbling into a ditch. That is not the way it happens. I didn't fall in love with Shirley . . . I *grew* into a close relationship with her. After the first surge of emotion was over, I began to develop a deep appreciation for this young lady. I enjoyed her sense of humor and her pleasant personality. I saw how she loved God and the better things of life. And little by little, I developed a desire to make her happy, meet her needs, provide a home for her, and live my life in her company.

But you should know that I don't always *feel* intensely romantic and loving toward Shirley. There are times when we are close and times when we are distant. We sometimes get tired and harrassed by the cares of life, and that affects our emotions. *However, even when the feeling of closeness disappears, the love remains!* Why? Because our relationship is not dependent on a temporary feeling; it's based on an unshakable commitment of the *will*. In other words, I have made up my mind to devote myself to Shirley's best interests, even when I feel nothing. I know the emotion of closeness will return when we have time to be together . . . when we're on vacation . . . when exciting events happen . . . when we're doing romantic things together. Sooner or later the feeling will return, and it will last for days. But when I get busy . . . when my mind is on other things . . . when there has been sickness or hardship in the family . . . it is likely that my emotions will become cool again.

Your emotions will fluctuate too. That's why you must understand that love is more than a feeling—it also involves a commitment of the will. You need an iron-fisted determination to make your marriage succeed, which will act like the engine of a train. It will keep you moving down the right track. On the other hand, the feeling of love is like a caboose, being pulled by the powerful engine at the other end.

A Final Word

If I had to put the message of this entire chapter in one sentence, I would say that real love is caring for another person almost as much as you do for yourself. That is exactly how the Bible describes marital love—it is becoming "one flesh" with another individual. The two of you actually become one person. It's much more than marrying an individual who will do something good for *me*. Rather, it is learning to love someone as much as I do my own flesh, and by marrying, we become united. That is the real meaning of love. If you have that kind of appreciation for another person, you are on your way to a happy home.

5

....

A Notion Called Emotion

We have discussed the canyon of inferiority, the dangers of conformity, the physical changes of puberty, and the meaning of love. Now it's time to get a better understanding of the emotions (or feelings) that often occur during the teen years. This topic is especially important because the changes that are about to occur in your mind will be almost as dramatic as those which will soon affect your body. Even now you are in the final flickering moments of childhood, and once you leave it, there can be no return.

Perhaps the best way to begin acquainting you with the emotions of adolescence is to relate a personal story about the saddest day of my own childhood. It began at eleven o'clock one morning when I was in the seventh grade. I was sitting in my school classroom when a boy near me motioned toward the door. I looked in that direction and saw my father beckoning me to come outside. He said we were going home and that I would not be returning to school that day. He didn't explain why.

As we walked to the car, I knew that my dad must have something awful to tell me. I could see the tension in his eyes, but I was afraid to ask him what had happened. Finally he turned to me and said, "Jim, I have some bad news for you and I want you to take it like a man."

I said, "Is it my mom?"

He replied, "No."

I said, "Then it's my dog, isn't it?"

My father nodded and then began to tell me the details. He said that my mother had been driving home in our car a few minutes earlier. My little dog (whose name was Pippy) saw her coming and ran in the street to greet her. He jumped on the side of the car as it passed, but apparently lost his footing and fell under the rear wheel. Mother then felt the sickening thud as the dog was struck and run over. Pippy screamed in pain, eventually lying motionless at the edge of the road.

Mother stopped the car immediately and ran back to where my dog lay. She bent over him and talked softly to the pup. He could not respond because his back was broken, but he could roll his little brown eyes to see who she was. When he recognized her, Pippy wagged his stubby tail in appreciation. He was still wagging that little tail when his eyes grew glassy in death.

Loss of a Friend

Now it may not seem so terrible to lose a dog, but Pippy's death was like the end of the world for me. I simply cannot describe how important he was to me when I was thirteen years old. He was my very special friend whom I loved more than anyone can imagine. I could talk to him about things that no one else seemed to understand. He met me on the edge of the sidewalk after school each day and wagged his tail to greet me (which no one else ever did for me). I would take him out in the backyard and we would play and run together. He was always in a good mood, even when I was not. Yes, Pippy and I had something going between us that only dog lovers can comprehend.

When my father told me this story of Pippy's death, I thought *I* was going to die. I couldn't swallow and I found it very difficult to breath. I wanted to run away . . . to scream . . . to cry. Instead, I sat quietly in the car with a great lump in my throat and a pounding sensation in my head.

I don't remember exactly how I spent that afternoon at home, although I do recall crying most of the day. I soon composed a poem in honor of my dog, entitled "To Pippy." It was not the greatest literary masterpiece of all time, but it expressed my feelings pretty well. The last four lines of the poem read:

My mother, she hit him, and oh how I cried
And softly and gently, a puppy dog died
And if there's a dog heaven, I know he'll be there
He's my poor little Pippy, with hair white and fair.

Later in the afternoon our family conducted a funeral service for the dearly departed dog. I dug a small hole behind the grapevine at the back part of our property, and as the sun was going down we put his stiff little body in the grave. Just before we covered him over, I reached in my pocket and retrieved a copper penny. I placed it on the bloody fur of his chest. Today I'm not sure why I did that. I guess it was merely my childish way of telling my pup that I loved him. And my father, who had told me to take the loss like a man, bawled like a baby on that day behind the grapevine. It was without question the saddest day of my childhood.

It is important to understand that there have been many more *significant* moments in my life since that day of Pippy's death. There have been more meaningful days, and certainly there have been greater losses than the one I experienced on that cloudy morning. However, there have been few sadder days even to this moment. Why? Because I was thirteen years old when Pippy died. That made it all seem so much worse.

The Strongest Feelings

You see, *everything* is felt more strongly during childhood, and especially during adolescence. Do you remember the first chocolate-covered cherry that you ate as a child? Can you recall how good it tasted, how the sweet flavor filled your mouth? I was given my first piece of this delicious candy in a doctor's office when I was six years old. I had fallen and split open my lip, which had to be stitched back together. I was such a "brave little boy" while being sewed up that the doctor gave me a chocolate-covered cherry as a reward. I had never tasted anything like that. I can still remember it today. For weeks afterward, the taste of that candy lingered in my mouth, and I longed for another one. I even considered splitting open my lip again just so I could be rewarded for additional bravery! Now obviously, candy is not that important to me today because my desires are not as strong in adulthood as they were in childhood.

Do you remember your first ferris-wheel ride? Do you remember your first trip to the dentist? (Who could forget that experience?) My point is that when you're young, the good things seem more astounding and the bad things are more intolerable. That's why the death of Pippy nearly killed me too.

Why have I told you this? What does it mean for your future? It means that your own feelings will probably become even more intense during the next few years. That's just the way adolescence is. Little things that won't bother you later in life will bug you as a teenager. Your fears will be more frightening, your pleasure will be more exciting, your irritations will be more distressing, and your frustrations will be more intolerable. Every experience will appear king-sized during early adolescence. That's why teenagers are often so explosive, why they sometimes do things without thinking and then regret their behavior later. You'll soon learn that feelings run deep and powerful during the adolescent years.

There are six other characteristics of emotions during adolescence that I would like to discuss with you briefly. We'll begin with a look at the "human yo-yo."

1. THE CYCLICAL EMOTIONS

It will help you to know that feelings tend to go from high to low to high to low. "Big deal," you say, "what does that mean?" It means that when you're depressed and unhappy and blue, when nothing is going right and life doesn't seem to be worth living, just hang tough for a few days. You won't remain depressed very long. Your circumstances will change and the sun will come up again. Sooner or later you'll wake up one morning and be glad you're alive. You'll bounce out of bed and whistle at the birds and wave at the flowers and sing "Zippity Doo Dah" all day long.

But I must warn you that this positive feeling won't continue either. You see, few people stay extremely happy or unusually depressed for very long. The usual pattern of all emotions is to move up and down, year in and year out. In fact, all of us are "yo-yo's" in that way. Therefore, when you're emotionally high, expect to come down; when you're rock bottom, expect to come up. That way you won't be surprised or depressed when sudden change occurs. Another way to describe these unstable feelings is to say that human emotions are *cyclical*. They occur in regular patterns and are influenced by the amount of sleep you've had, what kind of health you're in, and how things are going in your life. To tell the truth, the world is not the way it looks to you or me; our emotions distort or change the true picture somewhat. Now isn't that a heavy thought?

2. THE UNRELIABLE IMPRESSIONS

The second aspect of emotions that you should understand relates to the danger of impressions. An impression is an inner thought that you believe comes from God or somewhere unknown. For example, I know a young man who was driving down the street in his car, and he received the strong feeling that he would soon die. He seemed to "hear" this message deep within his mind: "Your life is almost over." He thought God was telling him to prepare for death. The sweat began to form on his forehead, and his mouth became dry. His hands got sweaty and his heart began to race. This fellow actually thought he might be enjoying the very last minutes of his life. In his distress, he nearly drove his car into a telephone pole (which would have proved the impression to be true, I suppose). But I can assure you that this young man is still alive today and is doing fine.

You may have impressions of many kinds, and if you believe them to be true, they can cause you to make wrong decisions. Some impressions might lead you to get married suddenly, or move to another town, or quit school, or join the Army. When these strong thoughts and feelings come, just remember that God rarely makes demands that require instant change. Give yourself a few days or weeks to look at all sides of the issue. And the more important the decision, the more carefully you should review the facts.

How to Know God's Will

I've said that impressions are not dependable as a basis for making quick decisions. How then can a young person know the will of God in a particular situation? How can he tell the difference between a spooky feeling and the genuine leadings of the Lord? Let me make five quick suggestions that will help with this task.

First, talk to another person about the decision to be made; discuss it with someone in whom you have confidence and with whom you can share your ideas.

Second, read the Bible for direction. God will talk to you through His Scriptures, and He will never ask you to do anything that contradicts His Word.

Third, watch to see which doors open and those that slam shut. If God is leading you in a particular direction, He'll work through what we call "providential circumstances." He will create opportunities for you to do what He wants. You won't have to "hammer down" the obstacles if God is involved.

Fourth, give yourself plenty of time to think. Don't make any big decisions while you're in a state of confusion. That's a good principle to follow throughout your life. When you're not sure what to do, avoid the final choice for as long as possible. You might have much greater confidence a few days later.

Fifth, pray for God's guidance and blessing and leading.

These are just a few suggestions to help you handle the impressions that will come during the next few years of your life. It's best to realize that these impulses are part of being a teenager. Don't let them lead you into anything that will damage the rest of your life. In other words, *be cautious!*

3. THE DECLARATION OF INDEPENDENCE

Now let's talk heart-to-heart about another emotional problem that usually arises during adolescence; we call it "the conflict between generations." This phrase refers to the irritation and harsh feelings that are likely to occur between you and your parents during the teenage years.

How can I predict that your mother and father

may become upset with you, and you with them in the years to come? The reason I know is because of the stressful changes that will soon occur in your relationship. When you were born, you were totally dependent on your parents for everything. Your very life was in their hands—you could do nothing for yourself: you couldn't roll over, you couldn't scratch your head, you couldn't even ask for food except by using that ear-shattering scream which God gave you.

But as you grew and learned and developed, you began getting free from that dependence. Soon you could hold your own bottle, and a little later you were able to sleep through the night without being fed. Then you learned to crawl, and soon you were walking. Each time you learned a new behavior, you were granted additional independence from your parents. Instead of having to be washed behind your ears, you became old enough to do the job yourself. Instead of picking up your blocks and making your bed and giving you every cent you needed, your parents allowed you to carry these new responsibilities. Later you learned to complete more difficult assignments and to think for yourself. With each step in the growth process you became more independent of your parents and they gained new freedom from their task of serving you. In a few years that process will be completed. You will be totally independent of your mom and dad, and they will be totally free of their obligation to serve you.

Completely Free

You had better prepare yourself for it: you will soon be your own boss. You will decide when to go out and when to come in, who to spend your time with, when to go to bed, what to eat, and exactly what you're going to do with your life. You'll decide whether you're going to worship God or ignore Him. Your parents won't be able to require anything of you because you will no longer be a child. In fact, your relationship with your parents should become more like a friendship, instead of them being your supervisors and disciplinarians. What I'm saying is that childhood begins with great dependence at birth and moves toward total independence at the far end of adolescence. During the same time, your parents are changing from servants to free people again. That's what childhood and adolescence and parenthood are all about.

What does this have to do with the conflict that I have predicted? Well, when a young person becomes fourteen, fifteen, or sixteen years of age, he sometimes gets a taste of independence and begins to demand his total freedom immediately. He wants to make his own decisions. He wants to run his own life. He begins to resent the control of his parents and sets out to prove that he is no longer a child. Mom and dad, however, know that their son or daughter is not ready for complete freedom (independence). He still needs their leadership in certain areas, and they are determined to give it to him. The result can be a painful struggle that may last for three or four years.

There is another dimension to this conflict. While the teenager is demanding complete independence from parental authority, he also insists on being very *dependent* in other areas. For example, he wants hot meals on the table three times a day and expects his shirts to be ironed and his doctor bills to be paid and his socks to be washed. In other words, he wants freedom without responsibility. That combination will not work. If a person is not yet ready to accept all the responsibilities of living, then he is not ready to handle unrestricted freedom either.

I'm saying that a million other families have fought over these issues of dependence-independence, and yours will probably have some trouble at the same point. If conflict occurs between you and your parents, I hope you'll remember that this tension is part of growing up. It doesn't mean that you don't love your mom and dad or that they don't love you. It's a natural struggle that occurs when you begin to demand more freedom than your parents know is healthy at the time. The best thing for you to do is talk to them openly about these matters. If you feel they are not giving you the independence *that is consistent with your age*, quietly say so. Tell them you feel you are old enough to make more decisions for yourself (and take the responsibility that goes with them). However, you must be reasonable. I advise you to yield to the leadership of your parents when they feel strongly about an issue. They do, after all, have your best interest at heart.

My Message

Let me conclude this point by telling you what I have said to my son and daughter with regard to this matter of independence. Perhaps your parents will adopt the same attitudes which are expressed in the message below:

First, I want you to know how much I love you. One of the greatest privileges of my life has been the opportunity to raise you . . . to be your father and watch you grow. However, you're now entering a new phase of life known as adolescence, which sometimes puts a strain on a loving relationship like ours. There may be times during the next few years when you will want me to give you more freedom than I feel you can handle. You may want to be your own boss and make all of your own decisions before I feel you are ready for that independence. This situation may create some friction between us, although I don't expect the conflict to be major.

If it occurs, however, I want you to know that I'm going to compromise as much as I can on each issue. I'll listen to your point of view and then try to understand your feelings and attitudes. I will not be a "dictator" who doesn't care about the needs or desires of the other person. In other words, my love for you will lead me to try to make you happy, if possible.

On the other hand, you can expect me to say "no" when my better judgment requires it. The easiest thing in the world would be to say, "Go ahead and do what you want. I don't care what friends you're with or what kind of grades you make in school. I'll stay off your back and you can do whatever you please." That would be a simple way to avoid all conflict and bad feelings between us.

But love demands that I do what is right, even if it is unpleasant. You'll soon learn that I have the courage to make those decisions when I must. Therefore, a moment of tension may occur in the coming years. But when it happens, I want you to remember that I love you and you love me, and we're going to remain friends through these difficult times. The world can be a cold and lonely place without the support of loving family members; that's why we're going to continue to care for one another in this home. And I think when you're reached your twenties and look back on these small conflicts, you'll appreciate the fact that I loved you enough to set you free gradually and as you were ready for additional responsibility.

If you are wise and mature, you'll accept this message from your parents during the years between childhood and adulthood. In other words, you will not issue your "declaration of independence" too early.

4. NO LONGER MOMMIE'S BABY

The desire for independence creates a strange sensitivity among adolescents about being seen in the presence of mom and dad. How odd it seems that a teenager should be embarrassed to sit in a restaurant or attend a basketball game with the parents who have raised him since birth! Nevertheless, *you* may feel the same way in the near future. It's not that you will suddenly dislike your mother and father, or that you are too good for them. The problem is that you want your friends to think you are grown up, and being seen with your folks seems like a babyish thing to do. This is especially true on Friday night, which is the traditional "date night."

How do I know about this embarrassing feeling? Because I *hated* to be seen with my parents when I was in junior high school. In fact, one of my most unpleasant experiences occurred the day I graduated from the eighth grade. My dad did what any proud father would have done—he brought his movie camera and took my picture in front of the school with my friends standing around. I remember that I resented him being there that day. I felt ridiculous with that camera pointed toward me. I didn't want to be a little kid anymore, who was being filmed by his daddy. That was what he would have done if I were three years old and had been given a new tricycle. When I see that movie today, I recognize the look of embarrassment on my face as a self-conscious eighth-grader.

These are some of the feelings you're also likely to have in the next few years. Of course, not everybody is the same. That's the fantastic thing about being a human being—we all differ somewhat, and you may never experience that feeling I described. But you're likely to be embarrassed when your folks are around your friends. It's not because you don't love them; you shouldn't feel guilty about that. It's because you want to grow up and you're worried about peer pressure. It's all a normal part of the adolescent experience.

Classroom Capers

Before leaving that thought, let me tell you something funny. My mother used this social pressure to make me shape up and behave properly in school. It began during the ninth grade, when I decided that it was more fun to be a goof-off than to work and study and learn. I had a couple of teachers who didn't know how to control their students very well, and my friends and I enjoyed disrupting their classes every day. I was having a great time laughing and joking, but my grades began to drop, as you would expect. I knew this wasn't right, but I was enjoying myself. My mother somehow knew I was playing games, even before the grades were distributed. I don't know how she found out, but she always seemed to know what I was thinking.

One day she sat me down for a little chat. She said, "I know what you're doing in school. Not only could you be making better grades, but I'm sure you're being disruptive in the classroom, too. I've been thinking about what I should do in response. I could punish you or take away your privileges, or I could visit your principal. But I've decided to do none of those things. In fact, I'm not going to do anything about your behavior. *However*, if your teacher or principal ever calls me to complain about the way you're acting, then the very next day I plan to go to school with you and sit by you in all your classes. I'll hold your hand as you walk down the hall and I'll be two feet behind you as you stand with your friends. I'll have my arm draped around your neck through the entire day at school. You won't be able to get away from me for a minute!"

Believe me, that threat scared me to death! I would much rather have had my mother beat me than go to school with me. Just the thought of that awful possibility straightened me out in a hurry. I couldn't run the risk of having my mama following me around at school! That would have been social suicide. My friends would have laughed at me for the rest of the year. I'm sure my teachers wondered why I suddenly became so cooperative during the latter half of ninth grade! Think about it. This tragedy could happen to you, too!

5. THE AGE OF CONFUSION

Now let's turn our attention to a fifth aspect of adolescent emotions that you ought to anticipate. If you are like most teenagers, you'll soon experience a time of confusion over what you believe. As a little child, you were told what was true, what the world was like, what values to keep, what to respect, and what to distrust. You accepted all these teachings without doubt or suspicion. When your parents said, "Santa Claus will come down the chimney at midnight," you fully expected the jolly fat man to be there.

As you progress through adolescence, however, it will be natural to examine each of the beliefs you have been taught. There will probably come a time when you will say, "Hey! Wait a minute. Do I really accept what my parents have said? Can I trust them to tell me the truth? Let's think this over before jumping to conclusions!"

This time of questioning is a very important event in your life as a young Christian. It can be the moment when you develop your *own* relationship with God instead of riding on the religion of your parents. On the other hand, it can be a distressing time because of the confusion it brings. That's why I mention it to you now, so that you won't be too upset during those days when nothing seems certain anymore. If you can keep searching for answers to the major questions of life, you'll eventually get satisfactory answers and solutions. And the chances are great that you'll discover that your parents were right in the first place.

6. THE SEARCH FOR IDENTITY

Closely related to this time of confusion will be another major event of adolescence, called the *search for identity*. This phrase refers to the need of each young person to know who he is. Let me ask how well *you* are personally acquainted with yourself. Do you know who you are? Do you know what you want in life? Do you know your own strengths and weaknesses? Do you know what you believe about God? Do you like the "image" your friends have of you? All of these questions relate to the search for identity.

Perhaps I can illustrate the importance of a well-defined identity by describing an individual who is poorly acquainted with himself. Marvin, as we'll call him, is one of four children, but he is neither the oldest nor the youngest in his family. His parents are extremely busy people and rarely have time to read to their children, or take walks, or play games, or build model airplanes. They do little except work day and night. Marvin thinks he is loved by his parents, but he doesn't feel very highly *respected* by them (or anyone else).

At five years of age, Marvin toddles off to kindergarten, where he spends most of his time riding the tricycles. A year later, he has some trouble learning to read. He has no idea why. The other students are also learning math much faster than he. Marvin rarely gets "happy faces" on his school papers. His teacher doesn't say "Nice work, Marv" in front of his classmates. And he knows his parents aren't too happy about his school performance either. He feels very dumb.

Junior high finally rolls around, and Marvin has no idea who in the world he is. He is not good at basketball or tennis or golf. He can't play a trumpet or a trombone or the drums. He doesn't draw or paint or create artistic projects. In fact, he has never done anything in his entire life that was worth mentioning or bragging about. He doesn't know what he wants to be after he grows up. In fact, he's not even sure he wants to grow up. What I'm saying is that a boy like Marvin has *no* sense of identity. If an English teacher asked him to write a one-page theme entitled "Who Am I," he couldn't compose the first line.

Marvin's problem is extreme, and it may not apply to you. However, most teenagers lack a sense of identity to some degree. If you find yourself in that situation, I urge you to shop around for who you are in the years that follow. Go out for various sports or try to learn to play a musical instrument or ask your mother to teach you to sew. You might also go to the counseling office of your school and ask to be given some interest tests and vocational inventories that will identify your likes, dislikes, and skills. Joining the Scouts can also introduce you to many new dimensions of your personality. By all means, don't let these years slip by without exploring the many possibilities that lie within you.

Becoming Men and Women

One more comment needs to be made in regard to your search for identity, and it has to do with finding the proper masculine or feminine role. You see, until now you've been a little girl or a little boy, but soon you're going to be a grown man or woman. Girls will begin taking on the behavior that is appropriate for women, and boys will adopt the very different style of men. But before these changes occur, you have to know what is masculine and what is feminine. Those differences are not as clear today as they were when your parents were children, and many young people have a very hazy sexual identity.

I heard a story the other day of a little boy and girl who had just been introduced. They were trying to decide what games to play, and the little boy said, "I have an idea—let's play baseball."

But the little girl said, "Oh, no, I wouldn't want to do that; baseball is a boy's game. It's not feminine to run around on a dusty vacant lot. No, I wouldn't want to play baseball."

So the boy replied, "Okay, then, let's play football."

She answered, "Oh, no, I wouldn't play football. That's even less feminine. I might fall and get dirty. No, that's not a girl's game."

He said, "Okay, I've got an idea. I'll race you to the corner."

She replied, "No, girls play quiet games; we don't

run and get all sweaty. Girls should never race with boys."

The boy then scratched his head, trying to think of what she might want to do, and finally he said, "Okay, then, let's play house."

She said, "Good! I'll be the daddy!"

I think this young lady was a little confused on what her role as a girl was supposed to be. She will probably have some important questions to answer in the years ahead!

Maybe you too will have to answer some questions about your sexual identity between now and adulthood. If so, the easiest way to learn how to play the role of your particular sex, whether it be man or woman, is to watch an adult whom you respect. Try to be like him or her. This is called *identifying* with another person. If it's your mother or your teacher or another adult of your sex, watch and learn how he or she acts. Quietly observe how he walks and talks, and gradually you will find that it will become natural for you to be something like your model, even though you're a unique individual. This process comes under the heading of the search for identity, and it is an important part of growing up.

It is fitting that we summarize this chapter with a discussion of identity. As you may have noticed, this *entire* book has been designed to acquaint you with yourself . . . to give you a better grasp of who you are and where you appear to be going. As I said in the first chapter, I hope you will use this book as a kind of springboard to gain even more information on this important topic. After you get to know yourself, you might discover that you are a rather nice person after all.

6

━━━━━━━━━━━━━━━━━━━━━━━━━━━━━━━━━

This Is How It Was
With Me

The final chapter of this book is very different from
the five which you have just read. In fact, it may be
different from anything you have *ever* read. But I
think you'll find this section very helpful and interesting.

You may be surprised to learn that I didn't write
the remainder of this book, nor did any other author.
The following text was actually taken from the recorded comments of four teenagers whom you will
soon meet. You see, I invited two boys and two girls
(all fifteen or sixteen years old) to come to my house
for the purpose of discussing the topics in this book.
They sat in our family room and shared their experiences, while a team of technicians recorded their comments on tape. Then we made copies of their remarks
and edited them slightly to make the discussion more
clear. The result is an eyewitness account of what it
feels like to grow up . . . from the viewpoint of four

young people who have recently had that experience.

It may take you a few minutes to get accustomed to reading a person's name before knowing what he or she said, but you'll soon adjust. It's almost like reading a stage play, although here the people are not merely acting. They are real flesh-and-blood teenagers, just like you are (or soon will be). Now let's meet these new friends.

Dr. Dobson: Hello, everyone, and welcome to my home. I've invited each of you here, as you know, to participate in a rap session . . . a free and easy sharing of ideas and experiences. I've been telling young people what it feels like to become an adolescent. I've described the fears and tears and jeers that often accompany this time of life, as well as the many exciting aspects of growing up. But *you* can do the job better than I can. You are closer to that experience, and we want each of you to share your feelings with us.

Let's begin with an introduction of my guests, starting with the young lady on my left.

Gaylene: Well, my name is Gaylene, and I live in Arcadia, California.

Dr. Dobson: How old are you, Gaylene?

Gaylene: I'm fifteen, but I'll be sixteen in June.

Dr. Dobson: You've told us your name and how old you are, but *who* are you, Gaylene? What kind of person are you? What things do you like?

Gaylene: Drama is my big thing. I'm in Junior Jesters right now, which is a drama group at our high school.

Dr. Dobson: How many plays have you been in?

Gaylene: We've done two plays this year, and I'm working on another scene right now.

Dr. Dobson: If you sat down to write a paper called "Who Am I?" would you say that your interest in drama is the most important thing we should know about you?

Gaylene: I think so, but even this interest is just a front, because the real me is hiding beneath it, somewhere.

Dr. Dobson: That's a very interesting point . . . we'll get back to it in a moment. Darrell, introduce us to yourself now.

Darrell: My name is Darrell, and I'm a junior at John Muir High School in Pasadena. I've just been elected Youth President at my church, which I think I'll have a lot of fun doing. And I'm sixteen years old.

Dr. Dobson: Do I understand that you've also been on the debate team at your school?

Darrell: Yes, and I love it. Ever since I was small I've liked literature and speech more than I did science and math. I guess I was just brought up that way.

Dr. Dobson: All right, let's move around the circle to the next person.

Ceslie: I'm Ceslie and I go to Pasadena High School. I've been thinking a lot about what I want to do when I grow up, and I think the most important thing to me will be getting married and having a family.

Dr. Dobson: How do you feel, Ceslie, about the people who say that having a family and being a housewife is not worthy of a woman's time? Have you ever thought about that?

Ceslie: I don't agree with them, but that's just for me, because I'm that kind of a person. I like doing housework and I like cooking and things like that.

Dr. Dobson: And how old are you?

Ceslie: I'm sixteen, going on seventeen.

Dr. Dobson: "Going to be"—each of you has pushed your age up a little bit. (Laughter.) Let me tell you something: in about fifteen years you'll be trying to hold it down, I can guarantee that! (Laughter.) Okay, Page, tell us about yourself.

Page: Well, I've lived here in Pasadena for about five years. I was raised in upper New York before my dad was offered a job out here. And I'm sixteen years old.

Dr. Dobson: And what are your interests?

Page: I enjoy most sports. That's my greatest love.

Dr. Dobson: I can verify that Page is a very good basketball player. As a matter of fact, Page and I played basketball together last Tuesday night, and I was very impressed by his jump shot from about twenty feet.

All right, we've now introduced each of your names and let people know something about your interests. I'm pleased to see that all four of you are acquainted with your own minds in that way. I meet many young people who have no keen interests in life; they don't play the piano, or get involved in debating or homemaking or basketball or drama or anything else. They have no goals, no purpose, and no reason for living. That can be a very sad situation, and it leads us to the first subject I would like to hear you discuss.

Earlier in this book I've tried to describe what feelings of inferiority can be like during the teen years. By that I'm referring to the belief by a young person that he isn't like by anyone . . . that he's a "loser" . . . that other people are laughing behind his back . . . that he is dumb or ugly or poor . . . that he doesn't do things as well as other people . . . that he is uncoordinated and clumsy . . . that all-in-all his life is one big disaster.

Those awful feelings of inferiority and inadequacy are very widespread among young people today. It affects adults too. I recently read a book written by comedian Woody Allen in which he said that his only regret in life was that he wasn't somebody else. He is not alone in those thoughts. Many teenagers would like nothing better than to crawl out of their skin and get into someone else's body.

The four of you sitting here with me this evening look like you've got it all together. You appear poised and relaxed and confident. But have you experienced those same feelings of inferiority? Have you ever been disappointed with the person you've become? Did any of you identify with the feelings I just described?

Gaylene: I sure did. They hit me during my first year of junior high school.

Dr. Dobson: Tell us about those difficult days.

Gaylene: Well, my dad died during the summer following my fifth grade in school. This death happened at a time when I was going through many physical and emotional changes, and I didn't handle it very well. So I entered junior high school without knowing who I was. I wasn't involved in anything and I had nothing to look forward to. It was a very difficult time for me.

Dr. Dobson: How did you overcome those problems?

Gaylene: My mother encouraged me to reach out, to get involved in as many activities as I could. Also, we got interested in Christianity during those years. Neither my mother nor my brother knew which way to turn, but my grandparents were very religious people. We moved in with them, and that's when I got involved in a Sunday school program, which helped a lot.

Dr. Dobson: Gaylene, you said this difficult experience occurred during your first year of junior high school. That doesn't surprise me, because the seventh and eighth grades are often the most upsetting period of a person's life. Feelings of inferiority frequently become the strongest during those two years, for some reason. I know hundreds of thirteen-year-olds who have concluded, "I'm worthless!"

Has anyone else fallen into this same "canyon of inferiority?"

Darrell: I did, although my situation was different from Gaylene's. I was editor of the school newspaper when I was in junior high school, which gave me some satisfaction and status. But my problems during that time came from church. I was "different" from my friends because I enjoyed schoolwork and speech and subjects like that, which more or less isolated me. I was not involved in the junior high activities at church. I remember one disastrous beach trip in particular. I had looked forward to going, but I came home and I just bawled. I really did. I felt so rotten because I was teased by people throughout the trip. I didn't know why everybody was picking on me.

Dr. Dobson: I'm interested in the attitude of your friends at church. Did they not respect you because you liked to study?

Darrell: Yes, that was a problem. In my group you were supposed to hate school. I was expected to say, "Forget it, teachers are a drag, school is lousy, and anybody who gets interested in schoolwork is a freak." Even now, most of my friends are bored with school, and they work only to get good grades. They say, "I'm not going to study this because it won't be on a test." And that's no good. So when I was in junior high, I was interested in my studies and tried to share my experiences and be open about them, but nobody else wanted to do that. They wouldn't open themselves like I did, and it caused problems for me. From that moment I didn't want to open myself either. It has taken about two years for me to get over these feelings and to start talking again in Sunday school and wanting to be free.

Dr. Dobson: How beautifully you stated it, Darrell. Young people get laughed at . . . teased . . . ridiculed for being open with each other. Their feelings are deeply hurt, and they come home and cry, as you did. Then they begin to "close down." The next day they will be more cautious . . . more reserved . . . more phony in their social contacts.

Have you ever wondered, Darrell, why your friends were not as open as you? It's likely that they had been burned in the same way you were, only earlier. They had already learned the dangers of being free and spontaneous. The result was a very uneasy, tense society where everyone knew he could be laughed out of school if he made one social mistake. What a tough way to live!

Darrell: The pressures are great. For example, everyone is supposed to be "cool" now. I mean, you're not expected to show your feelings or reveal your true self. If you do, someone will laugh at the tenderness, the softness, inside. Well, some people recognize that it is not worth it to be so cautious. I've even seen posters at our school that say, "It's not cool to be cool anymore." That's a quick way to rip yourself apart . . . to do more harm to yourself than others can do to you.

Dr. Dobson: A mother told me a few weeks ago that her seventh-grade daughter wakes up every morning at 5:30 and spends an hour thinking, "How can I get through this day without making a mistake that will cause people to laugh at me?" Isn't that unfortunate? Ceslie, I'll bet you've had some of those feelings, haven't you?

Ceslie: I remember the third week of my first year in junior high—it was a brand-new school for me. I knew a few people there, but I wasn't familiar with everything. I was really little. I was about four feet, nine inches tall, and that's very short. I knew this one girl at our school named "Big Bertha," and she was about five feet eight. Bertha was the meanest girl in school, and everybody would run away when she came around. I thought that was really awful . . . that people shouldn't run away from her. But one day we were going up the stairs and Bertha kicked me. I didn't like that, and I turned around and said something to her, and she kicked me harder. So I went home and didn't say anything to anybody, but I was so upset that I started crying. When I told my parents why I was crying they thought it was very unkind for a person to do something like that. So they called the principal and told him the story. Then they told me to treat Bertha just like I would treat anyone else, because the reason she was kicking me was because she was so embarrassed about being too large. It wasn't because she was really that mean; she just felt bad about herself.

Dr. Dobson: That was very good advice, Ceslie. You see, there are several ways people act when they feel inferior. Darrell mentioned one approach, which is to pull into a shell and be very cautious with your associates. Another way is to become very angry and resentful. Bertha took this second alternative. Can't you imagine how she felt, first by being called Big Bertha, and then by having everyone run away from her? Those two experiences would probably make *me* want to kick people too. Bertha had been hurt deeply, and that caused her to hurt you. How did you deal with Bertha the next day at school?

Ceslie: Well, she had a little group of friends; there were three of them that stayed together. Every time I saw them in the halls, I just smiled at them. I think it kind of made them mad at me, but I just kept smiling and they never did anything to me after that.

Dr. Dobson: Did you gradually come to accept yourself?

Ceslie: I think I'm still—

Dr. Dobson: You're still working on that?

Ceslie: Yes.

Dr. Dobson: You'll probably work on that the rest of your life.

Ceslie: I know.

Dr. Dobson: Most of us are working on the same project. Page, you started to say something.

Page: You're talking about people who get hurt by their friends. Well, when I was younger, I had an accident which crippled me for a summer. I had to wear these crazy-looking shoes to school. I had broken my leg and I had to wear elevated shoes. I didn't want to. I used to sneak my other shoes from my house and put them on later so people wouldn't laugh at me. This went on for a couple of years. People used to call me "Cripple," you know, and I really wasn't, but it hurt me to be teased. Even now I sometimes feel like, "Oh, I wish I could be like a certain person because he's so great, and boy, you know, all the people would really like me because I'd be such a great athlete." That's what I always wanted to be—somebody that would stand out and not be someone that people laugh at.

Dr. Dobson: Isn't it interesting that you all have had the *same* feelings? That is precisely my point. If we selected a thousand teenagers and asked each one the question I've asked you, nearly every person would tell us a story like those we've just heard—about being laughed at, about being different, about not being accepted by others. It's something everybody goes through today.

Now tell me why—why is it that we have to endure these difficult moments? Is there any way to avoid them?

Gaylene: I tried to solve my problems in the wrong way—by becoming friends with the "in" crowd. Like there were two different groups in my high school. There was this group that was into partying all night and then coming home late and lying to their parents; then there was the other group that tried to be more responsible. They believed that being wild wasn't going to fulfill their lives. But it wasn't easy for me to choose between these friends. I barged into the tenth grade and met people from the different groups and I didn't know exactly where to turn. There were more people in the rebellious group than in the responsible group, and that's just the way it is, and I didn't want to be laughed at and I didn't want to be rejected, and I didn't want everybody to think I was weird. So I just stood there, at a crossroads in my life, not knowing where to turn.

Dr. Dobson: Did you feel tremendous pressure to do things that you knew were wrong?

Gaylene: Yes! I was just a sophomore this year, and that's when you get most of the pressure; you get a tremendous amount.

Dr. Dobson: And that pressure can cause you to behave in ways that you know are harmful. I believe, for example, that most of the drug abuse in our country occurs because of the enormous pressure that Gaylene described. It's not the "high" that attracts kids—the problem is that they lack the courage to choose the right group. Did the rest of you have a similar choice to make?

Darrell: I had to decide whether or not I was going to follow the "rules" of my peers at school. I knew that if I didn't go along I would be "out."

Dr. Dobson: Give us an example of what you mean, Darrell. What kind of rules were you expected to follow?

Darrell: Well, like the "being cool" rule. You must not show your feelings because people might find something to laugh at. But there were other rules in almost every area.

Dr. Dobson: What about your clothes—did the group tell you what to wear?

Darrell: Yeah.

Dr. Dobson: How to talk?

Darrell: Yeah.

Dr. Dobson: And what slang to use?

Darrell: Yes. You sort of convince yourself after a while that it's what you really wanted anyway. I mean, you like to think that you're not conforming, that you just happen to like the same kind of Levis and shoes and sweaters that everyone else is wearing. But as styles change, you realize there must be some other force that is working on your attitudes. That other force is group pressure.

Dr. Dobson: How about the matter of drugs? Have any of you ever had anybody offer narcotics to you?

Gaylene: I have, in junior high. We had this bulletin board, and the librarian put up a poster about the dangers of taking drugs. While I was reading it, somebody came up to me and said, "Look nice, don't they?" Right there, they were offering the stuff to me! At the time (this was back in seventh grade), I didn't know much about medicines or anything, and when I told my mom about it, she was completely horrified. She said, "They never did that back in my day." She's always saying things like that.

Dr. Dobson: Don't you think it's tougher to be a teen-ager now than it was in the past?

Gaylene: Yes.

Dr. Dobson: There have always been pressures on young people, but now the drug problem and other dangers seem to be worse.

Have you ever been offered drugs, Ceslie, or have you ever seen them being used?

Ceslie: No, I've never hung around the wild group. I was always in the group that was quiet and —

Page: Gaylene said her mother couldn't believe drugs were actually available at school. Well, my parents have a hard time believing it too. But, you know, our society has changed. A new trend will come along and everybody wants to be part of the craze. But I worry about what will happen when we're older and we have our kids. How are we going to face this situation with our kids, if we've taken drugs and done wrong things? What answers can we give to our children?

Dr. Dobson: Those are good questions, Page, because that day will come very quickly. You'll find yourself trying to keep your own children from making the mistakes which worry your folks today.

Ceslie: I think many of our problems occur because we don't talk to our parents enough; we keep everything inside and we never talk to anybody who could help us. We talk to our friends who are having the same problems, but they don't have the answers and they don't know what to tell us. For example, Gaylene talked to her mom. That was probably the best thing she could have done. I would never have said anything to my parents, because they would have just blown up, you know, and gotten mad at the school. But I think that's very important—to have a relationship with your parents where you can talk openly to them, and not have to worry about how they'll respond. Then they can give you the answers that will be helpful to you.

Dr. Dobson: Two of you have now mentioned this matter of talking to your parents. How about the other two? Darrell, have you been able to talk to your mom and dad?

Darrell: I haven't had that much opportunity to talk to them because drugs have never been a problem with me. But I agree that adults can help us handle our difficulties if they're "tuned in." But sometimes they don't know what's going on. For example, I had one teacher in ninth grade who was out of touch. We were sitting in class one day and here comes this sweet, sickly smell of marijuana down the hall, as clear as could be. It drifted into the classroom and everybody knew what it was except the teacher (Laughter.) We were sitting there reading and looking at each other and just, you know, trying to hide our laughter, but the teacher was grading papers when all of a sudden she looked up and said, "My! What's that marvelous smell?" (Laughter.)

She had no idea why we broke up. It would have blown her mind, you know? She was the kind of teacher who would never give a thought to that kind of thing. But they're doing better at our school now. They have big drug-prevention programs, but even that's not going to be enough.

Dr. Dobson: How about talking to your parents generally about other things that bother you, Darrell. Can you express your feelings to them? Let's go back to that painful night when you went to the beach. (I had a night very similar to that, by the way). Did you come home and talk to your mom and dad about it?

Darrell: Yeah, I talked to my dad. Both of my parents were brought up in a very strict Christian environment, and my mom is still—well, I'm not saying she's narrow-minded, but because my dad has had more experiences, he's more flexible. He is a minister and so he knows how to counsel people with problems. He told me not to pay too much attention to all this laughter, and helped me understand it. But you know something? I discovered that I brought some of that scorn on myself. I'd worn this real goofy-looking thing—it wasn't funny, but it was goofy. (Laughter.) There's a difference between the two. You can cause people to make fun of you, and that is what I had done. Well, I got rid of that clothing the next day, you know?

Dr. Dobson: A person gradually learns to keep his peers from laughing at him. After he's been stung a couple of times, he finds out what's "dangerous" and what is not. Page?

Page: Sometimes I feel like I can talk to my father better than I can talk with my mother. Mainly, I guess, because he was a boy himself and he understands some of the situations that I'm going through. He always encourages me to choose the right kind of friends.

Dr. Dobson: Did you have to choose which group you'd join, just as the others mentioned?

Page: Yeah, and that is a very important choice. Some of my church friends began running with the wrong crowd, and they soon drifted away from God and began living the wrong kind of life. I'm thankful that I'm in a good group and that these things haven't happened to me.

Dr. Dobson: Well, Page, your comment raises an extremely important point. All of us are influenced by people around us. Even adults are swayed by social pressure. For this reason, the most critical decision you must make will involve the friends you choose. If you select the wrong group, they *will* have a bad influence on you. It is a certainty. Very few people have the self-confidence to withstand criticism by their closest friend.

Gaylene: I'd like to say that some of the nicest people are those who are not so popular with the "in" group. I'm dating a boy now who's in a wheelchair. He's extremely nice and has a fantastic personality. Some people look down on me for going with him. They say, "Well, why do you go with *him* when you could go out with someone who's normal?" I think that's unfair.

Page: I do too! But I feel the same pressure when I decide to ask a girl for a date. I know some of my friends are going to think she's not pretty enough for me, or something. And then I feel kind of low, you know?

Ceslie: Just recently, I've been realizing how important the personality of a person is. In my mind I'm always thinking, "What if I would marry that person; what would his reaction be to problems that we face? It's not going to matter what that fellow will look like at that time. Besides, he's going to get old anyhow. (Laughter.)

Dr. Dobson: That's not a very encouraging prospect, although I guess it's true! But you're right, Ceslie. I've seen a girl marry the best basketball player in school because he was such a great athletic hero. Ten years later, however, nobody could remember how the crowds cheered him. All they knew was that the guy couldn't earn a living and he couldn't make decisions and he beat the kids and screamed at his wife. Like you said, Ceslie, you need to look into the future and try to predict what your life will be like with a particular person.

Darrell: I'm in an interesting situation now. Junior high isn't that far behind me, but my little sister is already in junior high, and just last night she was really upset about the possibility that she might have to go to a different school next year. She talked to me about her worries, and I found myself saying the kind of things we've been saying tonight. As I was talking to her I said to myself, "What am I doing? This is an echo from about three years ago. I am my father and she is me." (Laughter.) You know, it's like my father's words were bouncing off the wall and coming back to her now. I could see that her problems weren't serious at all because I had been through them, and I kept saying, "Why can't she see? I'm giving her the clearest answers in the world." But yet when I was in that situation I had no idea at first what my father was talking about.

Dr. Dobson: You have to experience it before it makes sense, don't you? And, in that way, this tape recording may be a mystery to that listener who is between ten and twelve years of age who hasn't gone through the experiences we're describing. You may not fully understand what we're talking about, but when it happens to you, then it will be like turning on a light bulb in your head. You will remember this tape and our conversation about feelings of inadequacy and inferiority. When that happens to you, remember this very moment when I said that you *do* have great worth as a human being.

Gaylene: There's one inferiority complex that I had when I started seventh grade—my freckles! They show, despite the fact that I used to do everything that I could think of to hide them. My mom kept telling me, you know, don't hide them, they're beautiful. And like Darrell, I found myself telling another little girl the same thing a couple of weeks ago. She has freckles and they *are* beautiful, you know? I was telling her that people are going to tease her, but yet, she shouldn't be upset about it. In fact, freckles are valuable, because if you get pimples on your face, people can't tell the difference. (Laughter.)

Darrell: I don't have a bad acne problem. But it becomes worse at some times than other.

Dr. Dobson: Explain what acne is, for the benefit of those who don't know.

Darrell: It's well—it's completely physical. All these old wives tales are silly, like the one that says, "It's the wicked coming out in you." (Laughter.) It's a completely physical problem because you have more oil flowing through your system.

Dr. Dobson: Be more specific, Darrell. Tell us what it looks like.

Darrell: You get red pimples on your face and around your neck sometimes. They make you feel real ugly when the people you see on television, like Donny and Marie, seem to have an absolutely perfect complexion. You couldn't even find a speck of dust on the lens of the camera, you know? And when acne does flare up, it can be devastating—it really can knock you out. And, even though you tell yourself, "I know where my priorities are and I know that beauty isn't the most important thing," it still affects your self-confidence.

Dr. Dobson: You become sensitive, don't you?

Darrell: I heard this on Hollywood Squares—"What's the biggest problem that teens have to face up to?" The guy was just joking, and he said, "acne" because of the pun between "acne" and something being faced up to. Then the moderator says "Right!" And the audience laughed. But really, pimples affect your self-confidence. You have to go out into the world and say, "Here I am, friends, with these red bumps on my face." And it really can hurt. It's easy to say to yourself, "Okay, physical beauty isn't important." But it's not so easy to convince yourself of that when your face is covered with blemishes.

Dr. Dobson: I saw a study of hundreds of teenagers who were asked what they most disliked about themselves, and skin problems ranked at the top of the list. That is one reason I am so strongly opposed to Barbie dolls. I suppose every girl plays with Barbie dolls when they are young, and most people don't give a second thought to them. But what bothers me about Barbie is that she is physically perfect; there are no pimples on Barbie. Her skin is air-brushed; her hair has "body" (whatever that means); there is not an ounce of fat on her anyplace. In fact, the only flaw on Barbie's pink body is a little statement on her bottom that says she was made in Hong Kong! (Laughter.) And, you see, these dolls give a little girl an image of what she's supposed to look like when she becomes a teenager. Fat chance! That's not realistic.

Ceslie: It seems like you always get pimples right before a really special event at school. It never fails. You could look great two weeks before and don't have a single blemish, but then on the big date, it's measles time.

Dr. Dobson: It seems like there's a little gremlin somewhere who plants them on you at night.

Page: What we're saying is that people just have to learn to accept themselves, as they are. That's hard to do, and it's been hard for me. People are going to mock you and it's going to hurt, and sometimes you wish, just like I said before, "Why can't I be like that person who's perfectly clean and all the girls love him? Why can't I be like that? Nobody likes me." I think this is the most difficult problem junior high kids have to overcome—the acceptance of their bodies.

Ceslie: My mom once told me that beauty is something that grows inside of you, and that some people who are pretty on the outside don't take the time to work on their personality and character. Later on, those who were less attractive may even become happier because their inner beauty increases as they grow older.

Dr. Dobson: I wish everyone knew that, Ceslie. I saw another study that tended to prove what you said. The researchers identified the girls in college who were the most beautiful and those who were less attractive. Then they studied them for 25 years to see what happened in their marriages and later lives. Believe it or not, those who were less attractive tended to be more happily married 25 years later. So it's really wrong for everybody to feel like they have to be physically perfect.

Let me say, in summary, that *everybody* has something they don't like about themselves. For Page it was his shoes. He felt bad about having to wear those elevated heels. For Gaylene it was her freckles. For Ceslie it was being too short. For Darrell it was being studious instead of being athletic. If people were honest, they would all admit being embarrassed about some flaw that becomes a burden to carry throughout life. But it is unnecessary to worry! We all have great human worth, regardless of how we look. And that's the beautiful thing about Christianity. Jesus loves me, not because I am fantastically intelligent or handsome; He loves me simply because I *am*! What a comforting message! I don't have to do anything to earn His love. It is available to everyone as a free gift. For the person who has been damaged by feelings of inferiority that's quite a message.

—Break occurred at this point.—

Dr. Dobson: We have been joined by a new member of our group that I want you to get acquainted with now. Greg, tell us a little bit about yourself.

Greg: My name is Greg Nourse, and I work for One Way Library, a Christian cassette company. I came here tonight to help do the recording, but I thought it would be neat if I could join the group to discuss drugs from the point of view of a former abuser. I have been through the drug scene, so I thought it might be helpful to add a few of my comments.

Dr. Dobson: I agree, Greg. We can learn from your experience. As a place to begin, tell us how people get started taking drugs in the first place.

Greg: That's a very common question. Well, I started taking drugs becuase I was inquisitive, and bored, and because it was an easy way of being entertained. But once you start taking drugs, then it's not fun to feel normal anymore. I know about that feeling because I was loaded every day.

Dr. Dobson: What kind of drugs did you take?

Greg: I started with marijuana.

Dr. Dobson: Did that lead you to take other narcotics?

Greg: Not really. At least, there was no "addiction" which led me to take harder stuff. However, when you begin with marijuana, you are around drugs and around the people who use them. That's what led me to get in deeper.

Dr. Dobson: When did you begin experimenting with pills?

Greg: Well, I started getting loaded in grade school. I think I began with "reds," and then I took cocaine and about every psychedelic substance.

Dr. Dobson: All right, Greg, let's go back to the very first experience. Can you remember what happened?

Greg: Uh huh. My friend's big sister was a big "loader," and she used to make us roll up lids for her, and so we just—

Dr. Dobson: Excuse me. You have to explain your terms.

Greg: I'm sorry, a "lid" is a certain amount of marijuana, and you get it in a baggie or something, and then you have to roll it into cigarettes. The cigarette is called a "joint." Well, this girl used to make us sit there and roll up her "lids," which takes hours to finish. Sometimes she'd bring home a "brick," which is more than a lid. One day we were rolling joints when we decided to try one ourselves. We stole a couple of joints, and that's the first time I was loaded.

Dr. Dobson: Was it your idea or were you with somebody else who said, "Why don't we do it?"

Greg: It was my idea.

Dr. Dobson: You were the one who put the other guys under pressure, weren't you?

Greg: That's right.

Dr. Dobson: And you were soon taking other substances?

Greg: Yes. That went on all through high school.

Dr. Dobson: Tell us how you felt after you had taken a drug and then started to come down.

Greg: Coming down is horrible, especially when you've taken speed, which is an amphetamine. I always became really sick. Let me tell you that getting "strung out" on a drug is an awful thing, because you wake up in the morning and you know that you have to take that drug by the end of your day or you'll be sick. If you get the stuff, you make it through the day, but then your routine starts over again the next morning.

Dr. Dobson: What if you don't have money and you can't afford to buy what you need?

Greg: Well, it depends on what drug you're hooked on. If it's "speed" or heroin, you get terribly sick. With heroin you go through "withdrawals," which are awful. "Speed" is even more dangerous because it destroys your brain cells, it interferes with your circulation, causes your hair to fall out, and changes your entire personality. You become moody and sentimental; you'll cry over anything, because you get extremely depressed, especially when you're coming down. The same thing happens with "acid" (LSD). You become exhausted the day after taking it, and your head is kind of numb. The more you take LSD, the more it deteriorates you as a person. You become more introverted and less productive. The body was simply not made for these chemical influences.

Dr. Dobson: We hear people say that the psychedelic drugs make a person more creative and more knowledgeable of himself. Did you find that to be true?

Greg: Certainly not. You see things when you're on these drugs that you can't even remember. The experience seems neat at the time, but there are no benefits after you come down.

Dr. Dobson: I described a situation earlier where a young person was in a car with four of his friends who start passing around some reds. When he refuses to take them, everyone says, "Come on, Chicken, what are you, a baby? Are you afraid? Are you a coward? Everybody else is doing it. What's the matter with you?" What is he going to do at a moment like that? What suggestions can you offer to a young person who might someday be in that situation? He already feels inferior; he already feels that he doesn't like his freckles or the shoes he wears, or something else about himself. How is he going to handle that moment when it comes?

Greg: I'll admit that this guy is in a very difficult situation, especially if he's with people he respects and wants to be friends with. But he must make a decision in that moment that will be one of the most important choices he'll ever face. Once he starts taking drugs, after he says that first "yes," then he is in for years of trouble. So I suggest that he hang tough and refuse to go along. He should also start looking for some new friends, because the ones he has will probably be getting loaded more and more often. He can't stay in their group without also getting involved sooner or later.

Dr. Dobson: Greg, I would like you to comment on the role which inferiority plays in drug abuse, which we were discussing earlier. As you know, it

is my belief that the person who feels inferior—
the person who doesn't like himself—sometimes
uses drugs to escape. In other words, if he takes a
pill, then he can get away from himself for a few
minutes or an hour or two. Do you agree with
this viewpoint? Did feelings of inferiority play a
role in your own experience?

Greg: Absolutely. Inferiority played the most significant role in my case. People will always say that
they're not taking drugs to escape, but that's what
it boils down to. Drugs offer a quick way to get
away from those awful feelings of inadequacy.
However, those feelings are still there, waiting for
you when you get back.

Dr. Dobson: When did you begin to overcome your
self-doubts?

Greg: Believe it or not, they got worse when I graduated from high school. You see, most people
strive to be popular all through school, and I did
the same thing. But after your senior year, it just
kind of backfires. There's no one to be popular
for anymore. That's when feelings of inferiority
can become unbearable.

Dr. Dobson: Well, Greg, how did you get your life
back together? You were obviously in a mess, and
yet you sit here tonight, "clothed and in your
right mind."

Greg: Jesus Christ came into my life and made the
difference.

Dr. Dobson: Tell us how you found the Lord.

Greg: Well, I wasn't searching for God. I didn't feel
that I was searching for anything, but my friends
were talking to me about the Lord. Finally, it
wasn't anything they said—it was just kind of a
revelation from God, I knew I needed Him. I
asked, with what little faith I had, for Him to

come into my life, and He did. And I knew immediately that He had.

Dr. Dobson: When you came to Jesus, did you get rid of your drug problem once and for all?

Greg: Uh huh. I did. When a person comes to the Lord, he feels clean inside and like a new person. Jesus said, "Peace I leave with you, my peace I give unto you; not as the world giveth, give I unto you. Let not your heart be troubled, neither let it be afraid."

Dr. Dobson: Greg, I appreciate your sharing your experience with us and giving us this personal testimony. I'm sure many young people will be helped by it.

Greg: Thanks for letting me tell my story. Now I'll get back to the recording.

Dr. Dobson: I would like the four of us to discuss another extremely important aspect of adolescence, and I'm referring to the physical changes that occur during the early teen years. It's not uncommon for kids to be frightened by what is happening to their bodies. Did any of you experience those fears during early adolescence?

Gaylene: I did. I began changing very early, in the fourth and fifth grades. This scared me because my mom hadn't told me what to expect.

Dr. Dobson: She hadn't prepared you for these changes?

Gaylene: No, because she figured it wouldn't happen until the sixth or seventh grade. When it happened early I didn't know what was going on. And I hit the panic button!

Dr. Dobson: What kind of fears did you have, Gaylene? Did you wonder if you were abnormal in some way, or if you had a terrible disease?

Gaylene: I thought I was going to die. I really did. I was in school and ran to the nurse's office in tears. That's how scared I was. And she didn't know what was wrong because I was too hysterical to explain it to her.

Dr. Dobson: Your honesty is very helpful, Gaylene, because it will encourage others who are listening not to be afraid when their own physical changes begin to occur. They should know that the growing-up process is controlled by the pituitary gland in the brain. At a certain time and at a certain age, it sends out chemical messengers called hormones which produce these sudden changes that can be so terrifying.

Gaylene: Well, you know, when you said that we shouldn't be scared, that's easy to say, but how can a person help being scared? For example, when I found out I was allergic to bees, my mom said, "Just don't be frightened of them." But I can't help it. When they come near me, I run in the opposite direction. I'm deathly afraid of them. It didn't help me get over my fear when my mother told me not to worry.

Dr. Dobson: There is a difference, though, Gaylene. You really *do* have something to fear from bees because you are allergic to their sting. However, the thing I want to convey to those who are pre-teenagers is that they *don't* have anything to fear from the physical changes that are occurring. It's a natural process that happens in all healthy people. Darrell?

Darrell: I was very small in junior high. Well, I guess most of the guys are shorter than the girls in junior high anyway.

Dr. Dobson: That's right.

Darrell: I'm beginning to catch up with the others now, but for awhile I was sensitive about my

height. But I wasn't the only one who was uncomfortable, because the physical changes of adolescence coincided with physical education as a
special class in junior high. In other words, at the
time when you were most conscious of your body,
you had to take showers and expose yourself to
everyone in the locker room.

Dr. Dobson: Absolutely!

Darrell: I know I worried more about going to P.E.
than any other class, even though it was the easiest class of the day. I enjoyed playing basketball
and other sports, but I was sensitive about my
body, and letting others see it. Everyone felt the
same way. That's why P.E. caused a lot of problems.

Dr. Dobson: Darrell, you've shown great insight by
your comment. P.E. classes *do* cause many worries for junior highers. Those who haven't ma-
tured are very sensitive about their babyish bodies, especially when they notice that everybody
else looks more like an adult. This causes *tremendous* anxiety, especially for the kid who is teased
by his friends. I've had students say to me, "Kick
me out of school, flunk me, send me to Siberia,
put me in jail, do *anything*, but I'm not going to
take a shower after P.E. again!" And I understand
their feelings.

Gaylene: When I was told that I would have to dress-
out for P.E. and then take a shower, I became
very tense and worried. I didn't even want to go
to school that day. I pulled every trick in the
book on my mother. I got sick during the evening
beforehand. I tried everything. But she made me
go to school anyway. All the girls felt the same
way I did, and it was funny, because the towels
they gave us weren't big enough to cover us.
(Laughter.) We were really supposed to dry on
the towels, but everybody wrapped them around

themselves, and then tried to dress and undress with the towel still in place. We didn't want anybody to see what we looked like. And oh! It was terrible!

Dr. Dobson: And everybody was going through the same thing.

Gaylene: Everybody was embarrassed and selfconscious! (Laughter.)

Dr. Dobson: Have the others of you had the same kinds of feelings and fears?

Ceslie: I used to dress in the showers! (Laughter.)

Dr. Dobson: You see, you're all in the same boat. Page, the same problem?

Page: Yes, it happened to me too.

Dr. Dobson: These experiences are more painful, of course, for those who have those old feelings of inferiority. That one problem seems to pop up everywhere.

Page: Another thing that makes boys uncomfortable is not being very strong. A lot of guys are into the "Mr. Muscleman" thing, you know, and if you're skinny they laugh at you and make fun of you. I'm not the strongest kid in the world, you know, so I always wanted to work out; I wanted to build up my muscles, so I could be like the group. I think this is why I felt inferior.

Dr. Dobson: And you see, before puberty occurs— before you grow up—your muscles are like a child's muscles. They become more powerful and more like a man's muscles shortly after the growth spurt occurs. Therefore, the boy who is late in maturing is likely to be weaker. That makes it difficult for him, because his friends are playing football and doing things that take strength. Power is very important to junior high-

ers, and those who haven't developed feel power-
less for awhile. That can bring on the feelings
Page just described.

Gaylene: There's something else that embarrasses me.
Boys and girls have a separate P.E. class, of
course, but sometimes we all get on the same
courts at the same time. Then you're really
scared, because the boys are over there and
they're dressed up for P.E. and you're dressed out
over here. We may be playing basketball and
they're playing volleyball. And the tension is terrible! You're trying to do your best, but I'm no
basketball player—I'm short, sometimes I even
feel crippled (laughter)—and you sure don't want
to be laughed at. All the girls are trying to impress the boys and the boys are trying to impress
the girls. It's a tense time.

Darrell: When the guys and girls are on the same tennis courts or something like that, that's when the
bullies (the guys who want to build themselves
up), take advantage of those times. When I was
in junior high they would sneak up behind a guy
and just go like this (demonstrates a downward
pull)—just yank down his trunks. (Laughter.) Of
course, the poor guy would grab them and pull
them right back up. But, really, I lived in terrible
fear of that happening to me. I would never show
my face ever again anywhere if that ever happened, so I spent half my time playing tennis and
the other half looking over my shoulder. As a result I'm not too good of a tennis player! You have
to be careful, you have to watch out, not to put
yourself in a vulnerable position. You can't do too
much to avoid being humiliated, but you can
help a little.

Page: Being with a girl is a prime time for some guys
to get revenge on you, to say something about
you or your family. It can hurt really bad.

Dr. Dobson: What I hear you saying is that you are most cautious when you are around the opposite sex. When the girls are around the guys and the guys around the girls, that's when you are most vulnerable. And that's easy to understand.

I'm inviting Mr. John Styll to join us now. He's also a technician who's here to run the recorders. However, this discussion we're having is so fantastically stimulating that the technicians keep wanting to jump in and offer their two bits. So why not? John, welcome to the group.

John: Thank you.

Dr. Dobson: You've been ten feet away for the past hour, and I know you have some thoughts on the subject of inferiority.

John: I just wanted to say that many of us become supersensitive about the way we look, you know, like "I'm too fat," or "I'm too skinny." I had the same problem because I never thought I was very handsome. Then I'd see people who were very attractive and I'd want to be like them. I always wanted to have black hair, for example, and I was never satisfied with the way I actually looked. Since then, I've learned that God made everybody the way they are for a reason, and He doesn't make mistakes. I've met a few people who understood that principle and refused to let their imperfections bother them. I know a girl, for example, who has to wear crutch-type braces to walk. She has some kind of crippling disease—I don't know what it's called—but her legs are very thin and she can't walk on them. Nevertheless, that girl is one of the most beautiful people I know. She is such a glory to God, because *she* knows that she's supposed to be like that. Consequently, she builds people up and makes them feel happy. That makes her feel happy in turn. It's really a wonderful thing. But people often get

so concerned with the way they look that they
fail to understand that God can use them just the
way they are. God has a purpose for each one of
us, and it's our duty to find out what His purposes are and then to fulfill them.

Dr. Dobson: That's the secret of self-confidence,
John. However, a person's tiny flaws can cause
him to withdraw in a corner, sit with his mouth
shut, and never use the talent God has given him.

John: That can certainly happen. It's funny. I never
thought of myself as being anything special, as a
leader-type person. But in high school I emerged
that way. You know, somebody asked me to get
involved and I said "yes." So I was the editor of
the high school newspaper and became involved
in many other activities. But I had to be willing
to take that first step.

Dr. Dobson: And as your confidence grew, your ability grew. This is a principle that I would like all
our readers to understand. You may think you
have no ability or skills, but your real problem is
that you merely lack *confidence*. Let me tell you
about the low point in my life. I was asked to
share my Christian testimony at a camp when I
was in high school. I only intended to talk five
minutes, so I memorized a frozen little speech.
But the young person who spoke before me
talked for about thirty minutes without taking a
breath. His words were perfect, and the more he
talked, the more frightened I became. I knew I
didn't have that much to say. When I finally
walked out on that stage and looked at all those
people my same age, my mind checked out for
lunch. I stood there completely blank with nothing to say. All of those students sat in icy silence
and stared at my red face. It was one of the most
frightening and discouraging moments in my entire life, as I fished for something to say. Today, I

speak all over the United States and receive thousands of invitations which I don't have time to accept. The difference between that first disaster and today's success is a matter of *confidence*.

John: That first experience probably made you want to succeed even more, didn't it?

Dr. Dobson: It did, but it took me five years to get over it. I can't describe how painful that failure was at the time, but as you said, John, the Lord made use of that terrible moment. It gave me a desire to learn how to handle a speaking opportunity.

Gaylene: Talking about confidence, the same thing was true for me in drama. I didn't think I was capable of acting. I thought I had to be some spectacular TV star. I signed up for a drama class, and every day the teacher kept hounding me and two other girls to get up on the stage and act. But I didn't have any confidence and I just kept hiding around the corner and being very shy. Finally I gave it a try. It was very hard the first time, but gradually I began to believe in myself. Now it's become easy for me.

John: Everybody's basically the same. In my work I meet people who are well-known and important, but they're just ordinary people, just the same as we are.

Dr. Dobson: All right, suppose you lack self-confidence. Where do you start to build it? Any suggestions?

John: Everybody, I don't care who they are, has something that they can do. You may be able to make a bigger mudhole in your backyard than anybody. (I'm not suggesting that you do anything negative or destructive.) But everyone has some undeveloped abilities, and you should identify them and cultivate them. My sister felt she could draw fairly well, so she just practiced over and over, and now art is her thing, you know? I don't think she was born an artist, but she developed her skill. My other sister is bananas over gymnastics. She's not as good as that little Russian girl—

Dr. Dobson: Olga?

John: Yeah, Olga Korbut, yeah.

Dr. Dobson: The principle that you are giving us here is one that I really believe in and tried to describe earlier. If you feel inferior and inadequate and think you don't have anything to offer, start shopping around for your hidden abilities and skills. Try to identify your own strengths and the interests that you can cultivate and then pour all of your resources into them. You'll soon be feeling better about yourself.

Page: Well, what if you try something that is really new and then you fail at it? That causes people to put you down. Aren't you worse off than before?

John: Not necessarily, because it doesn't really matter what other people think. The fact that you had the courage to try something that you didn't understand shows a lot about you, about the kind of person you are.

Page: Yeah, but sometimes your parents encourage you to plunge into something unfamiliar, and then you do lousy, you know? Then you feel low and discouraged. They shouldn't push you into doing something that you feel is not right for you.

Dr. Dobson: You're right, Page, but look at it this way. A little child who is taking his first step has to fall down before he can learn to walk, right? He would never learn to walk if he weren't willing to fall down in the beginning. And with us,

the fear of falling can keep us from trying anything new. It can keep you bottled up because
you're afraid to run a few of those risks. With a
little confidence you can achieve something that
will make you proud of yourself. That's what
your parents are hoping for. Ceslie, I want to
hear from you.

Ceslie: One of the things that is just terribly hard for
me to do is to get up in front of a group of people
and sing or talk or do anything. A year ago, I
tried out for drill team at our school. (The drill
team performs at football games and other school
activities.) This is a big deal, and everybody tries
out for it, but many don't make it. You have to be
good to be chosen. The first time I tried out I
was so scared that I thought I was just going to
flub the whole thing. But if you practice something often enough and you've worked hard to
learn it, then it becomes easier, like Gaylene said.
That's what happened to me, and I was chosen
for drill team. Last night was my final performance for drill team, and I wasn't even scared to go
on the field. However, one year ago I thought I
was going to pass out in the middle of the performance. It was just practice that pulled me
through.

Dr. Dobson: It increased your confidence, didn't it?

Ceslie: Right.

Dr. Dobson: Will this success make is easier for you to
try something new the next time?

Ceslie: Yes, I think so.

Dr. Dobson: Because you faced fear, didn't you?

Ceslie: Uh huh.

Dr. Dobson: If you had done what you really felt like
doing, you would have run away?

Ceslie: Right.

Dr. Dobson: I know a great track star—as a matter of fact, he won three gold medals in the Olympics. He said that before every track meet he wants to run out of the stadium. Also, I'm told that Wilt Chamberlain would go into the bathroom and throw up before every basketball game in college. That tremendous tension, that fear, can keep you sitting at home in a chair, crying perhaps, instead of using those skills that God has given you.

Darrell, I don't want to put you on the spot, but I wonder if you'd tell us in closing what Jesus Christ means to you.

Darrell: Well, we sometimes sing a song in Christian Minstrels which includes this idea: no matter what a person does for himself, he is certain to fail unless there is teamwork between him and God. That's the way I feel. Jesus Christ is always there to help me . . . to give me confidence . . . to be my friend. Of course, He expects me to do my part of the teamwork also, to develop the talents He's given me and take the opportunities that He sends my way. This relates to what we've been discussing tonight. It is our responsibility to apply these principles that have been suggested, but even if we make all the right moves, we still can't make it on our own. Speaking for myself, I depend on the partnership with God. He is always there to support me, especially during times of struggle. Not only do I have other people and friends to help me, but Christ is also working within me. That's what He means to me.

Dr. Dobson: That is beautifully said, and there is a Scripture verse that expresses the same thought. It says, "Except the Lord build the house, they labor in vain which build it." That means that you can create your own empire and become the world's greatest authority on a given subject and

earn a fortune, but unless God is in it, you have
wasted your time. God wants us to say to Him, "I
don't have much, but my life is yours. Please take
it and bless it."

Ceslie: This has helped me so much through the
years. I know the Lord accepts me the way I am
because He is the One who made me the way I
am. I don't have to worry about the way I look or
the way I talk in front of people. The Lord knows
me and has my life in His hands.

Dr. Dobson: Isn't that neat? God's acceptance is *un-
conditional!* Even if I'm not the most admired
person in the world; even if I'm not the most
beautiful or intelligent person; even if I don't
own a fortune; even if I haven't set any athletic
records; even if I have fallen short of what I expected to accomplish, and even if I disappointed
other people . . . nevertheless, I am just as worthy in the sight of God. Page, do you believe this
is true? Is Jesus Christ real to you?

Page: Yes, He is. But there have been times when I've
drifted away from the church and from the Lord,
and I can tell you right now, without Christ in
me, I am totally different in every way. But when
Christ is in control, it is just like having a friend
with you who helps all the time.

Dr. Dobson: Gaylene, in conclusion, would you say
that it has been fun growing up, or has it been
difficult and painful?

Gaylene: Both. It's been fun, but at the time I
thought, "Oh, I'm not going to live through it."
But now that I look back on all the experiences, I
wish I were twelve again so I could do it all over.
I can tell you there would be a lot of things I
would want to do different.

Dr. Dobson: That's probably a pretty good place to
end our conversation. I want to thank all of you

for being here with us this evening and for being so honest and for sharing some of your private feelings with us. I hope these discussions have been useful to those who are listening. Perhaps they will help each person avoid the familiar pitfalls and enjoy some of the blessings that life has in store for you. Thank you again, and goodbye.

The Final Message

Well, I think we've covered the subjects that you should know about the approaching adolescent experience. We've talked about inferiority, conformity, puberty, romantic love, and emotion. All that remains is to offer one or two final suggestions that may help you cope with the pressures we've been discussing.

Today Is Not Forever

First, there is a tendency during the adolescent years to feel that "today is forever"—that present circumstances will never change—that the problems you face at this moment will continue for the rest of your life. For example, many teenagers who feel inferior and unpopular in school usually believe that they will always be unloved and rejected. They cannot imagine a situation different from what they experience in school each day. In truth, however, the teen years will pass quickly, and will soon be nothing more than a dim memory. Those friends (and enemies) who share your classes will graduate in a few months and will move across the country. Once that has occurred, no power on earth could bring them back together as things are today. The mini-society at your junior high or high school will shatter like humpty-dumpty, never to be reassembled again.

So if you find yourself unhappy for one reason or another during adolescence, just hang tough—things will change. That fact is one of life's certainties, and understanding it can help you cope with an uncomfortable circumstance. *Tomorrow will be different.*

Normality Will Return

Let me offer another encouraging message about the adolescent years which can be summarized in three words: *normality will return.* By that I mean that you're about to go into a hectic, topsy-turvy world which will make new demands and will confront you with many new challenges. (Remember that I said you may even feel once in a while like you're hanging by your heels?) When these stressful moments arrive . . . when you ask a girl for a date and she turns you down, when you don't get invited to the party being given for the popular people, when your parents seem to hassle you over everything you do, when pimples and blackheads attack your forehead like an army of insects, when you wonder if God is really there and if He genuinely cares . . . in those moments when you're tempted to give up, please remember my words: "normality will return."

Just as I was able to predict many of the adolescent experiences which came your way, I can also predict with certainty that this stressful time of life will pass. In some ways, adolescence is like a tunnel that has a known beginning and end. As long as you stay on the road and keep your car moving forward, you can expect to emerge at the other end. Likewise, the anxieties and struggles you have experienced will soon disappear, and a new set of adult pressures will take their place. That's life, as they say.

Your Very Best Friend

The final (but most important) advice I can give you is to remain friends with Jesus Christ during the years ahead. He loves you and understands all of your needs and desires. He will be there to share your brightest days and your darkest nights. When you face the important issues of life (choosing a mate, selecting an occupation, etc.), He will guide your footsteps. He gave us that assurance in Proverbs 3:6, which says, "In all thy ways acknowledge Him, and He will direct thy paths." What a comforting promise!

I want to thank you for taking this ride through adolescence with me. Even though you and I have never been introduced, I feel that this book has permitted us to become good friends. In fact, I wish that you would write and tell me about your own teen experiences. Unfortunately, I receive more mail than I can possibly answer, but I read every letter that comes.

I trust that God will bless your life, and I hope to meet you someday.

Dr. James Dobson

OTHER MATERIALS FOR THE FAMILY
By Dr. James Dobson

BOOKS:

Dare to Discipline, Bantam Books, 1977, Tyndale House Publishers, 1970.

Hide or Seek, Self-Esteem for the Child, Fleming H. Revell Publishing Company, 1974.

What Wives Wish Their Husbands Knew About Women, Tyndale House Publishers, 1975.

The Strong-Willed Child, Tyndale House Publishers, 1978.

CASSETTE TAPE RECORDINGS:

Preparing for Adolescence, Vision House Publishers (One Way Library). This album contains six cassette tapes, designed to help the pre-teenager prepare for the experience to come. The book you have just read was based on these original six recordings.

Preparing for Adolescence Growth Pak, Vision House Publishers, (One Way Library). This package includes the tapes described above, the *Preparing for Adolescence* book, a workbook for preteens, and two cassette tapes designed to help parents use these materials and cope with the adolescent challenge.

Discipline: From Cradle to College, Vision House Publishers (One Way Library). This album contains six cassette tapes, based on the concepts discussed in *Dare to Discipline* and *The Strong-Willed Child*.

Kids Need Self Esteem Too, Vision House Publishers (One Way Library). This album contains six cassette tapes, and presents the ways parents and teachers can maximize self-confidence in children.

What Wives Wish Their Husbands Knew About Women, Vision House Publishers (One Way Library). This album deals with the basic content of the book by the same name, although it contains speeches, radio interviews, and counseling conversations. Dr. Dobson has called this album "The most important work of my professional life."

Focus on the Family, World Publishers. This twelve-tape album discusses twenty different topics of relevance to family life, including parent-child relationships and marital harmony.

These items are available in local bookstores, or can be ordered by writing Box 952, Temple City, California 91780. Dr. Dobson can also be contacted through that address, although he regrets he is unable to respond to requests for personal consultation.

ABOUT THE AUTHOR

JAMES DOBSON, PH.D., is Associate Clinical Professor of Pediatrics at the University of Southern California School of Medicine, and Director of Behavioral Research in the Division of Child Development, Children's Hospital of Los Angeles. He also serves as co-director of a nationwide Collaborative Study of Children Treated for Phenylketonuria (PKU), a ten-year investigation being conducted in fifteen major medical centers in the United States. Dr. Dobson is personally committed to the integrity of the American family, and has dedicated his professional life to its preservation. His first book for parents and teachers, *Dare to Discipline*, has now sold over a million copies, and his second, *Hide or Seek*, is also a national bestseller. He is a licensed psychologist in the State of California, and is a popular speaker in family life seminars, churches and schools throughout the country. As a devoted Christian husband and the father of two children, Dr. Dobson's own family ranks at the top of his system of priorities and values. A popular television guest, Dr. Dobson has made several appearances on the "Dinah Shore Show," "A.M. America," Tom Synder's "Tomorrow Show," and five appearances on Barbara Walters's "Not for Women Only," with Dr. Benjamin Spock, Dr. Lee Salk, and Dr. Helen Derosis. Dr. Dobson and his wife, Shirley, live in Arcadia, California.

DAHL, ZINDEL, AND BRANCATO

Select the best names, the best stories in the world of teenage and young readers books!

☐	22690	8 PLUS 1 Robert Cormier	$2.25
☐	14944	PHOEBE by Patricia Dizenzo	$1.95
☐	20250	CHARLIE AND THE CHOCOLATE FACTORY Roald Dahl	$2.25
☐	20206	CHARLIE AND THE GREAT GLASS ELEVATOR Roald Dahl	$2.25
☐	12153	DANNY THE CHAMPION OF THE WORLD Roald Dahl	$1.95
☐	20172	THE UNDERTAKER'S GONE BANANAS Paul Zindel	$2.25
☐	15185	THE WONDERFUL STORY OF HENRY SUGAR AND SIX MORE Roald Dahl	$2.25
☐	12966	DON'T SIT UNDER THE APPLE TREE Robin Brancato	$1.75
☐	22722	BLINDED BY THE LIGHT Robin Brancato	$2.25
☐	22540	THE GIRL WHO WANTED A BOY Paul Zindel	$2.25
☐	14657	THE PIGMAN Paul Zindel	$2.25
☐	23150	I NEVER LOVED YOUR MIND Paul Zindel	$2.25
☐	14836	PARDON ME, YOU'RE STEPPING ON MY EYEBALL! Paul Zindel	$2.25
☐	20759	MY DARLING, MY HAMBURGER Paul Zindel	$2.25
☐	20170	CONFESSIONS OF A TEENAGE BABOON Paul Zindel	$2.25
☐	23124	WINNING Robin Brancato	$2.25
☐	23098	SOMETHING LEFT TO LOSE Robin Brancato	$1.95

MS READ-a-thon–
a simple way
to start youngsters reading.

Boys and girls between 6 and 14 can join the MS READ-a-thon and help find a cure for Multiple Sclerosis by reading books. And they get two rewards — the enjoyment of reading, and the great feeling that comes from helping others.

Parents and educators: For complete information call your local MS chapter, or call toll-free (800) 243-6000. Or mail the coupon below.

Kids can help, too!

TEENAGERS FACE LIFE AND LOVE

Choose books filled with fun and adventure, discovery and disenchantment, failure and conquest, triumph and tragedy, life and love.

☐	22605	**NOTES FOR ANOTHER LIFE** Sue Ellen Bridgers	$2.25
☐	22742	**ON THE ROPES** Otto Salassi	$1.95
☐	22512	**SUMMER BEGINS** Sandy Asher	$1.95
☐	22540	**THE GIRL WHO WANTED A BOY** Paul Zindel	$2.25
☐	20908	**DADDY LONG LEGS** Jean Webster	$1.95
☐	20910	**IN OUR HOUSE SCOTT IS MY BROTHER** C. S. Adler	$1.95
☐	20907	**HIGH AND OUTSIDE** Linnea A. Due	$1.95
☐	20868	**HAUNTED** Judith St. George	$1.95
☐	20646	**THE LATE GREAT ME** Sandra Scoppettone	$2.25
☐	23447	**HOME BEFORE DARK** Sue Ellen Bridgers	$1.95
☐	13671	**ALL TOGETHER NOW** Sue Ellen Bridgers	$1.95
☐	20608	**A HOUSE FOR JONNIE O.** Blossom Elfman	$2.25
☐	14306	**ONE FAT SUMMER** Robert Lipsyte	$1.95
☐	14690	**THE CONTENDER** Robert Lipsyte	$2.25
☐	13315	**CHLORIS AND THE WEIRDOS** Kin Platt	$1.95
☐	23004	**GENTLEHANDS** M. E. Kerr	$2.25
☐	20537	**HEY DOLLFACE** Deborah Hautzig	$1.95
☐	20474	**WHERE THE RED FERN GROWS** Wilson Rawls	$2.50
☐	20170	**CONFESSIONS OF A TEENAGE BABOON** Paul Zindel	$2.25
☐	14225	**SOMETHING FOR JOEY** Richard E. Peck	$2.25
☐	14687	**SUMMER OF MY GERMAN SOLDIER** Bette Greene	$2.25